Assessment and Diagnosis for Organization Development

Assessment and Diagnosis for Organization Development

Powerful Tools and Perspectives for the OD Practitioner

Edited by
William J. Rothwell, Angela L.M. Stopper,
and Jennifer L. Myers

CRC Press
Taylor & Francis Group
Boca Raton London New York

CRC Press is an imprint of the
Taylor & Francis Group, an **informa** business

A CHAPMAN & HALL BOOK

CRC Press
Taylor & Francis Group
6000 Broken Sound Parkway NW, Suite 300
Boca Raton, FL 33487-2742

© 2017 by Taylor & Francis Group, LLC
CRC Press is an imprint of Taylor & Francis Group, an Informa business

No claim to original U.S. Government works

Printed on acid-free paper

International Standard Book Number-13: 978-1-1380-3334-4 (Paperback)

Library of Congress Cataloging-in-Publication Data

Names: Rothwell, William J., 1951- author. | Stopper, Angela L. M., author. |
Myers, Jennifer L., author.
Title: Assessment and diagnosis for organization development : powerful tools
and perspectives for the OD practitioner / William J. Rothwell, Angela
L.M. Stopper, Jennifer L. Myers.
Description: Boca Raton, FL : CRC Press, 2017.
Identifiers: LCCN 2016035602 | ISBN 9781138033344 (pbk. : alk. paper)
Subjects: LCSH: Organizational change. | Organizational
effectiveness--Evaluation.
Classification: LCC HD58.8 .R6845 2017 | DDC 658.4/06--dc23
LC record available at https://lccn.loc.gov/2016035602

Visit the Taylor & Francis Web site at
http://www.taylorandfrancis.com

and the CRC Press Web site at
http://www.crcpress.com

William J. Rothwell dedicates this book to his wife,
Marcelina V. Rothwell. She is the wind beneath his wings.

Angela L.M. Stopper dedicates this book to her unbelievably supportive,
flexible, and always-in-her-corner husband, Benjamin C. Stopper, the State
College Tribe, and her Chapter 8 Crew. "You all make me a better person."

Jennifer L. Myers dedicates this book to her niece, Nevaeh and her nephew,
Leonardo. Always follow your dreams and use your talents to make the
world we live in a better place. I love you both more than you know.

Contents

Preface

This book comes from a real-world perspective and provides insights from those practitioners and consultants practicing organization development (OD) assessment and diagnosis today. OD assessment and diagnosis is not based on a medical approach that begins with diagnosis and ends with prescriptions or therapy. Instead, OD engages clients to build change leadership initiatives customized to meet client-defined problems and implement client-defined solutions. OD is not about a consultant telling a client company what to do. Instead, it is about an OD professional guiding client companies on their journeys toward the best end point for their particular situation. This book will address that journey.

To do so, the theory and foundational principles of OD are covered. However, much of this book provides applications to the real world of OD consulting practice. Although this book is grounded in sound academic theory, the chapters are laid out in a practitioner-focused way, containing real-world themed vignettes and tools that individuals can use to help guide organizational assessment and diagnosis efforts in their own or client organizations.

The Audience for this Book

This book is for current or aspiring OD consultants and managers who wish to apply facilitative approaches to change. It addresses organizational assessment and organizational diagnosis for those who work inside organizations (that is, internal OD consultants) and those who work outside organizations (that is, external consultants). It should also interest others, such as human resource professionals and operating managers, who have reason to manage change in organizational settings.

Overview of the Contents

This book comprises nine chapters.

Chapter 1 introduces the concepts and overall theory related to diagnosis and assessment for OD. It briefly describes the difference between OD and performance consulting. This chapter sets the stage for the remainder of the book, engaging the reader and inciting their interest in the topics and learning to come.

Chapter 2 discusses the methods that can be used in an OD assessment and diagnosis from the organizational-, group- and individual levels and provides some tools that practitioners can use at each of the levels. Central to this is the link between an organization's strategic plan and the assessment. This chapter includes two vignettes, one focused on diagnosing with a clearly understood mission, vision, and strategic plan in place and the other focused on diagnosing without an articulated and written mission, vision, and strategic plan. This chapter also includes some discussion to help OD practitioners clarify his/her role with clients and with themselves. It ends by spending time engaging the reader to think about how to measure success when performing assessment at different levels, as well as a worksheet to engage practitioners in creating a strong self-assessment of their OD intervention in order to promote continued growth and learning.

Chapters 3 and 4 build on the discussions from previous chapters by describing diagnostic models from which OD practitioners select or synthesize data. Diagnostic models are very important in organizational assessment and diagnosis. Chapter 3 starts with a comparison between open and closed systems and then goes into detail regarding the key features of open systems. Open systems are discussed first, because most diagnostic models are based on open systems. Guidelines for identifying and applying open systems models are discussed, and numerous real-world themed vignettes are included, focusing on (1) identifying and synthesizing an open systems model, (2) the application of an open systems model, and (3) the OD effectiveness model. This chapter closes with examples of data collection tools employing open systems models.

Because diagnostic methods are built on models, this chapter serves as a foundation for subsequent chapters on planning, gathering, and analyzing data.

Chapter 4 helps OD practitioners understand models that address environmental forces and organizational readiness. The topics include force field analysis and practical guidelines for assessment. In addition, this chapter explores the use of models to address the readiness of an organization (that is, Likert System 1–4, High Performance Programming Model) and practical guidelines for models for highly ready organizations (that is, Appreciative Inquiry and The Great Place to Work Model). This chapter includes numerous vignettes focused on (1) addressing the readiness of an organization, (2) the application of Appreciative Inquiry, and (3) the application of the Great Place to Work Model. This chapter ends with tools pulled from each vignette, including questions to ask, tips for following up on the results, and key takeaways for OD intervention development.

Chapter 5 introduces the importance of dedicating time and resources for planning assessment and feedback. It introduces key concepts and literature to help the reader understand organizational assessment and feedback and provides a model that has proven to be a valuable tool for assessment, planning for feedback, and organization improvement. This chapter includes a real-world themed vignette and provides a tool to help practitioners plan for successful assessment and feedback.

Chapter 6 specifically focuses on the tools and techniques needed for collecting and analyzing data in organizational assessment and diagnosis. In this digital age, we all know that you can collect a plethora of data on any number of topics. But what makes useful data (information) different from noise is its meaningfulness related to the current situation. This chapter will explore the importance of individualized data collection to make the information gathered meaningful and actionable to your team. It will also provide insights into the numerous tools that can be used for data collection, describing the positives and challenges with each and giving practitioners all of the information they need to design a solid data collection plan. This chapter includes a real-world vignette focused on increasing employee participation in OD engagements, discussion on real time and simulated observational data collections, and tools to help practitioners write strong interview and survey questions. It ends with a checklist to help practitioners craft a strong behavioral observation worksheet.

Chapter 7 describes how to provide data collected during organizational assessment to the client. Key to this point is for the practitioner to have good facilitation skills so the organization's perspective and point of view emerge in a collaborative discussion about the data, the gaps, and the strategic outcome desired. This discussion is followed by another one on the next step in assessment, diagnosis, and action planning. This chapter discusses action planning where a change model involving multiple stakeholders, planning, and execution of the plan is created.

This chapter focuses on tools to use to communicate the diagnosis and assessment in a way that involves the client and provides insights while not falling into prescriptions like performance consulting. The chapter outlines this process, gives examples of reports, and gives tips on facilitating a feedback session to move to a collaborative plan of action. It closes with a Feedback and Action Planning Worksheet, designed to allow practitioners a quick reference guide to use when designing a feedback session with clients, as well as links to Project Management and other tools needed for success in this step of the OD assessment and diagnosis process.

Chapter 8 challenges readers to think about the ways in which the organizational assessment and diagnosis process can go wrong. Four real-world themed vignettes are included that dramatize how mistakes can be made at each of the start gates (planning, collecting and analyzing data, feeding back data, and action planning). Steps to avoid the challenges are then discussed. This chapter ends with a Challenges Quick Reference Tool, outlining the chapter information in bullet format and the steps used to overcome the said challenges.

Chapter 9 concludes this book. What future challenges are likely to affect assessment and diagnosis for OD in the twenty-first century? How can organizational leaders prepare for these challenges? This chapter describes possible future trends and offers ideas on how to prepare for these challenges. This chapter ends with a worksheet for meeting the future challenges in OD assessment and diagnosis, providing practitioners with a tool that they can use to plan for meeting the stated challenges.

Acknowledgments

The editors thank the many people who helped make this book possible. That includes chapter authors as well as those who looked over the manuscript to improve it.

Of special note, we thank Kathleen E. Wolfhope for her early contributions to this project and Aileen G. Zaballero for her intrepid Project Management skills.

About the Editors

William J. Rothwell, PhD, SPHR, SHRM-SCP, CPLP Fellow, RODC (see www.rothwellandassociates.com) leads a graduate emphasis in organization development at the master's and PhD levels at Penn State University. He had 20 years of full-time work experience in HR in both government and business before he became a consultant and university professor 18 years ago. Best known for his extensive and high-profile consulting work in succession planning, organization development, and talent management with numerous organizations in the United States and around the world, William J. Rothwell is a frequent speaker or keynoter at conferences and seminars around the world. He has authored, coauthored, edited, or coedited more than 300 books, book chapters, and articles. His most recent publications are *Organization Development in Practice* (ODNETWORK, 2016), *Mastering the Instructional Design Practice* (Wiley, 2016, 5th ed.), *Practicing Organization Development* (Wiley, 2015, 4th ed.), *Effective Succession Planning* (Amacom, 2015, 5th ed.), *The Leader's Daily Role in Talent Management* (McGraw-Hill, 2015), *Career Planning and Succession Management* (Praeger, 2015), *Organization Development Fundamentals: Managing Strategic Change* (ATD Press, 2015), *The Competency Toolkit* (HRD Press, 2015, 2nd ed., 2nd vol.), *Creating Engaged Employees: It's Worth the Investment* (ATD Press, 2014), *Optimizing Talent in the Federal Workforce* (Management Concepts, 2014), *Performance Consulting* (Wiley, 2014), the *ASTD Competency Study: The Training and Development Profession Redefined* (ASTD, 2013), *Becoming an Effective Mentoring Leader: Proven Strategies for Building Excellence in Your Organization* (McGraw-Hill, 2013), *Talent Management: A Step-by-Step Action-Oriented Approach Based on Best Practice* (HRD Press, 2012), the edited three-volume *Encyclopedia of Human Resource Management*

(Wiley, 2012), *Lean But Agile: Rethink Workforce Planning and Gain a True Competitive Advantage* (Amacom, 2012), and *Invaluable Knowledge: Securing Your Company's Technical Expertise-Recruiting and Retaining Top Talent, Transferring Technical Knowledge, Engaging High Performers* (Amacom, 2011).

Angela L.M. Stopper, PhD, is the director of program innovations and executive education at the UC Davis Graduate School of Management where she oversees the development and delivery of innovative management and leadership development programming for the school. In addition to her work at UC Davis, Dr. Stopper is also an adjunct assistant professor of education at Penn State, where she has developed and is teaching a course for the master of professional studies in organization development and change. Over her career, Dr. Stopper has worked in numerous client-facing positions at Penn State in the Outreach and Online Education Departments and the Penn State Smeal College of Business. Dr. Stopper's current research focus is global talent development. Working with the Association for Talent Development, the research team is investigating trends and challenges, and how formal, informal, and social learning play in this area. Dr. Stopper is the author and coauthor of multiple publications and presentations focused on global talent development, online education, service marketing, change leadership, and strategic visioning and leadership. Her most recent publications include Association for Talent Development: *Building a Talent Development Structure without Borders* (2015, Alexandria, VA: Author, Product Code: 791504-WP), and "Measuring and Addressing Talent Gaps Globally" (*Global HRD*, 32[1505], 1–18) with W. J. Rothwell, A. L. M. Stopper, and A. G. Zaballero. Her past research projects include numerous internal and external corporate needs assessments, workshop development and facilitation in the United States, Saudi Arabia, and China, consulting projects focusing on executive coaching, and research papers in the areas of learning preferences of a generationally diverse workforce, cross-generational collaboration, and using distance learning in noncredit adult education programs. Dr. Stopper holds a BS in marketing and international business, an MS in workforce education and development, and a PhD in workforce education and development with a concentration in human resources and organization development, all from the Pennsylvania State University.

Jennifer L. Myers, PhD, is a practitioner in the field of human resource development and organization development for the public sector. She is also graduate faculty at Penn State, teaching an organizational diagnosis course in the master of professional studies in organization development and change. Dr. Myers holds a PhD from the Pennsylvania State University in workforce education and development, specializing in human resource development and organization development. She received her master's degree from Boston University, Massachusetts, and is also a graduate of the Federal Law enforcement Training Center (FLETC), Georgia. Prior to transitioning to her current position, she served as an instructor for the Professional Personnel Development Center (PPDC) at Penn State. Dr. Myers is also an Operation Enduring Freedom (OEF) veteran and is a recipient of numerous service awards, some of which include the Air Force Expeditionary Service Ribbon with Gold Bolder, Meritorious Unit Award, and multiple Commendation Medals. Her current research interests are employee engagement, organization development, and strategic planning. Dr. Myers is the author and coauthor of multiple publications and presentations focused on engagement, diversity, healthcare, and career development. Dr. Myers' most recent publications include the following: Zaballero, A. G., and Myers, J. L. 2014. Engaging the best people. In W. Rothwell, A. G. Zaballero, and J. G. Park (Eds.), *Optimizing Talent in the Federal Workforce*. New York: Management Concepts Press. Baumgardner, C. Z., and Myers, J. L. 2014. Creating an engaged culture. In W. J. Rothwell (Ed.), *Creating Engaged Employees: It's Worth the Investment*. Alexandria, VA: ASTD. Wolfehope, K., and Myers, J. 2014. Leadership and the effects on employee engagement, *Journal of Knowledge and Human Resource Management*, 6(13). Alzahmi, R. A., and Myers, J. L. 2013. Identifying performance gaps through needs assessment. In W. J. Rothwell (Ed.), *Performance Consulting: Applying Performance Improvement in Human Resource Development* (pp. 342–344). San Francisco, CA: John Wiley & Sons. Imroz, S. M., and Myers, J. L. 2013. Application of SWOT Analysis. In W. J. Rothwell (Ed.), *Performance Consulting: Applying Performance Improvement in Human Resource Development* (pp. 305–307). San Francisco, CA: John Wiley & Sons.

About the Authors

Hyung Joon Yoon, PhD, is currently an assistant professor of human and organizational learning at the George Washington University (GWU), Washington, DC. Prior to joining GWU, he worked as an assistant professor and program coordinator for the Human Resource Development Program at Al Akhawayn University in Ifrane, Morocco. He also served as graduate faculty at Penn State, teaching an organizational diagnosis course in the master of professional studies in organization development and change. He holds a PhD in workforce education and development from Penn State and has gained multinational experiences in countries such as the United States, South Korea, and Morocco as a researcher practitioner. Dr. Yoon was bestowed with the Individual Greatness Award (Franklin Covey Greatness Award) in recognition of the creation of measurable change in an organization in 2006. He has presented his research findings at international and national conferences more than 30 times in seven countries. He has developed or codeveloped career development models and assessment tools through research, including the Hope-Centered Model of Career Development (HCMCD), Hope-Centered Career Inventory (HCCI), the Human Agency Based Individual Transformation (HABIT) model, and the Assessment of Human Agency (AHA). He is certified as a Senior Professional in Human Resource (SPHR), and Career Development Facilitator Master Trainer. He serves the National Career Development Association (NCDA) as trustee-at-large (2016–2019).

Julie D. Staggs is an associate client partner in the Global Education Practice of Korn Ferry Hay Group, based in the firm's Atlanta, Georgia office. She is an experienced higher education professional who has worked both for and with higher education for more than 25 years. From admissions and marketing to curriculum development/delivery and talent management, she has assisted institutions in reaching their strategic goals. Her engagements have included working with various universities in strategic planning; culture/org design; inclusion practices; competency modeling; new program planning, development, and launch; marketing strategy; and evaluation. She has directed all project phases, including research, planning, hiring, training, implementation, and evaluation. Previously, she consulted for Fortune 100 companies in the areas of corporate training, innovation, and strategic planning. Her consulting at Corporate Executive Boards (CEB) focused on innovation and strategic partnering besides teaching in the Corporate Leadership Council's (CLC) Leadership Academies. Her combination of higher education and corporate experience provides a broad perspective for each project. These combined areas of expertise enable her to develop and deliver customized solutions for institutions. Earlier in her career, she worked with Adecco as a placement specialist in Washington, DC, with a focus on placing recent college graduates. As a member of Korn Ferry's Global Education practice, she works with institutions around the globe to design and implement leadership development strategies and programs across the institution with students, staff, and administration. She received her bachelor's degree from Converse College, South Carolina, in music theory and religion and her executive masters of business administration degree, with a concentration in leadership, from University of Georgia. She is working on her doctorate of education in higher education management at the University of Georgia's Institute for Higher Education. She also serves on the Board of Trustees for Converse College.

Lindsay Weissberg, JD, is a practitioner in workforce development for the federal government. She holds a juris doctor (2009) and a master of public health (2010) from the University of Pittsburgh, Pennsylvania. She graduated with distinction from her juris doctor program, receiving the Excellence in Health Law and the Order of the Barristers awards. While a student, she was the executive editor of the *Pittsburgh Journal of Environmental and Public Health Law* and coauthored articles related to the intersection of the law and public health priorities. Prior to graduate school, she worked in the international affairs and public policy arena in Washington, DC. She graduated cum laude from George Washington University, Washington, DC, in 2003 with a bachelor of arts in international affairs and minors in Spanish and political science. Her current professional interests relate to employee engagement and retention, workplace diversity, supervisor development, and strategic planning.

Advance Organizer

William J. Rothwell

Complete the following Organizer before you read this book. Use it as a diagnostic tool to help you determine what you most need to know about assessing and diagnosing organizations—and where you can find it in this book *fast*.

The Organizer

Directions

Read each item in the Organizer below. Circle a *true (T)*, a *not applicable (N/A)*, or *false (F)* in the left column opposite each item. Spend about 10 minutes on the Organizer. Be honest! Think of assessing and diagnosing OD as you would like it to be—not what some expert says it is. When you finish, score and interpret the results using the instructions appearing at the end of the Organizer. Then be prepared to share your responses with others you know to help you think about what you most want to learn about assessing and diagnosing organizations. If you would like to learn more about one item in the Organizer, refer to the number in the right column to find the chapter in this book in which the subject is discussed.

Circle Your Response for Each Time Below			OD Consultants Should	Chapter in the Book in Which Each Topic is Covered
T	N/A	F	Be able to explain the difference between organizational assessment and diagnosis.	1
T	N/A	F	Be able to explain the difference between organizational assessment and diagnosis as conducted by OD practitioners and as conducted by performance consultants.	1
T	N/A	F	List organizational assessment/diagnostic models as roadmaps to guide the process.	2
T	N/A	F	Apply an open systems approach to organizational assessment and diagnosis in OD.	3
T	N/A	F	Apply force field analysis in organizational assessment and diagnosis in OD.	4
T	N/A	F	Apply a model that has proven to be a valuable tool for assessment, planning for feedback, and organization improvement.	5
T	N/A	F	Use tools and techniques needed for collecting and analyzing data collected for organizational assessment and diagnosis.	6
T	N/A	F	Feedback data collected during organizational assessment to the client.	7
T	N/A	F	Think about (and avoid) ways that the organizational assessment and diagnosis process can go wrong.	8
T	N/A	F	Plan for 10 predictions about the future of organizational assessment and diagnosis in OD.	9
			Total	

Scoring and Interpreting the Organizer

Give yourself *1 point for each T* and a *0 for each F or N/A* listed above. Total the points from the *T* column and place the sum in the box opposite to the word *Total* in the Organizer. Then interpret your score as follows:

Score

10–9	Congratulations! Give yourself a grade of A. You may be doing an effective job of organizational assessment and diagnosis from an OD perspective.
8–7	Give yourself a grade of B. You are doing many things right in organizational assessment and diagnosis from an OD perspective. But room remains for improvement. Focus your attention on those.
6–5	Give yourself a grade of C. You are muddling through. You should focus on improving how you carry out organizational assessment and diagnosis using an OD perspective.
4–3	Give yourself a grade of D. You are below average in organizational assessment and diagnosis from an OD perspective. Act to improve it!
2–0	Give yourself a grade of F. You are failing in your approach to organizational assessment and diagnosis. *Take immediate action to improve it!*

Chapter 1

Introduction and Overview of Diagnosis and Assessment for Organization Development

William J. Rothwell

Contents

1.1 Introduction

Organizational assessment, often associated with *organizational diagnosis*, is the systematic process of examining how well an organization is functioning. It is the single most important step in any helping relationship—and consulting is a helping relationship—because the issues surfaced in assessment become the basis for subsequent action. If the assessment is performed poorly (or not at all), then subsequent action will not be targeted properly. If that happens, then any subsequent action may worsen conditions rather than improve them.

This chapter addresses several important questions:

- What is organizational assessment and organizational diagnosis?
- Who conducts organizational assessment and diagnosis?
- When is organizational assessment conducted?
- Where is organizational assessment conducted, and how does context affect the assessment process?
- Why is organizational assessment conducted?
- How is organizational assessment conducted?

1.2 What Is Organizational Assessment and Organizational Diagnosis?

Organizational assessment is a systematic investigation of an organization (Lusthaus et al. 2002; Levinson 2013). It may focus on outputs (results); it may focus on processes (throughputs); it may focus on inputs; it may focus on feedback systems; or it may focus on any or all of those. It may focus on the organization's performance within the context of its industry, community, nation, or its global position. Organizational assessment may focus attention on specific problems or strengths but may also examine how well an organization functions within a larger context outside the organization.

Organizational assessment implies measurement. But organizational diagnosis implies a problem-solving focus by which an organization is compared to something else (Levinson 1976; Weisbord 1978; Howard and Associates 1996; Harrison 2004). Diagnosis, often associated with the medical profession, suggests comparing something wrong (like a sick patient) with a desired or desirable standard (like a healthy person).

1.3 Who Conducts Organizational Assessment and Diagnosis?

Organizational assessment or diagnosis may be carried out by internal or external consultants. It may also be carried out by managers, workers, or other organizational stakeholders. It can also be carried out by stakeholders working as internal and/or external consultants.

Who conducts the organizational assessment is important because ownership and buy-in usually stems from participation and a say in decision-making. If consultants conduct assessment, then only consultants have ownership in the process and results. If managers conduct assessment, then only managers have ownership in the process and results. Deciding who should conduct the organizational assessment is a strategic issue because it determines how much other stakeholder groups may be invested in the process and its results.

1.4 When Is Organizational Assessment Conducted?

Organizational assessment is not (and should not be) conducted at only one time; rather, it should be conducted on a continuing basis.

But consultants of all kinds often face a challenge when they propose to conduct assessments. The reason is simple. Managers, who may pay the bill for consultants, assume that they already know what the problem or issue is, and what should be done about it. With a strong bias for action and a compelling sense of urgency, managers may believe that conducting assessment is too time-consuming, too expensive, and delays harvesting the benefits of action. Managers may tell consultants to skip any systematic assessment and go right into implementation because the managers believe they already know what is wrong or what strengths should be leveraged to advantage.

In organization development (OD), assessment should at least be conducted at two points in time. The first point is upon the consultant's initial entry to the organizational setting. If consultants are brought in from outside, they may not be familiar with the organization and must be oriented to it promptly. That process is called a *mini-scan*, but it really involves orienting the consultant to the client's world. A second form of organizational assessment, typically associated with what most consultants mean when they use the term, is to gather information about the issues affecting the organization. It may be carried out comprehensively or situationally. A *comprehensive organizational assessment* seeks to place the organization in context and to gather information about how well the organization is performing. It may focus on solving organizational problems or building on organizational strengths. A *situational organizational assessment* seeks to uncover information about a *felt need*—that is, a feeling that a need exists for change.

Examples may help clarify the meanings of these terms.

Suppose an internal consultant is called in to help one facility. The consultant may not be familiar with the facility and may need to learn about it quickly to become helpful. The consultant may seek information about that the facility. The same need would also exist if an external consultant were called in to help the same facility, since neither the internal consultant nor the external consultant may be familiar with the facility. Becoming oriented to the facility is a mini-scan.

But consultants are rarely called in to organizational settings for no reason. There is always a reason for the consultant to be there. If top managers, who are paying the consultant's fee, ask for the consultant to examine the organization broadly to find areas for improvement (or areas of strength to leverage), the consultant may undertake a comprehensive assessment of the organization. A comprehensive assessment can be difficult to organize, because there are so many areas that may be the focus of attention. For instance, consultants could look at the following:

- Organizational history
- Organizational mission
- Organization strategy
- Organizational structure
- The organization's relationship to external groups such as industry, community, nation, suppliers, distributors, customers, unions, and other groups
- Organizational performance against targets
- Organizational performance against best practices
- Organizational performance against legal issues
- Organizational performance against common business practices

As organizing the assessment is the biggest challenge in a comprehensive assessment, consultants may rely on various models of assessment to focus attention. Clients are briefed on the model(s) that consultants may use and, if clients will pay for such an assessment, the consultants are then positioned to move forward with a work plan.

A third form of organizational assessment runs during implementation. After all, OD change efforts may extend over long timespans. During a three-year implementation, for instance, there may be need to assess problems coming up during implementation, prioritize them, surface solutions for them, and develop action plans to implement those solutions. Assessment can be ongoing and overlapping with evaluation.

As a simple example of the approach described in the previous paragraph, I was involved with a multiyear OD intervention. As part of that process, I conducted a weekly survey on Friday by e-mail. Results were fed back on Monday in staff meetings as a continuing way to assess how the implementation was going, and how any issues surfacing during implementation could be addressed.

More common in consulting is that managers already feel they know what the problem is (or the strength to be leveraged) and will ask consultants to gather information about the issue. For instance, managers may say *our turnover is too high.* To them, turnover is the problem, though good consultants know that turnover is really a symptom of some other root cause(s). In this example, turnover is a *presenting problem* (i.e., the symptom that led a client to call in a consultant). But turnover is not the real problem; rather, it is a consequence of other problems (i.e., root causes that lead to the turnover).

But consultants entering an organizational setting must take care to avoid biasing results by how they approach organizational assessment. As a simple example, if managers complain about turnover, consultants may choose not to ask people "what do you think about the high turnover?" To take that approach is to jump to the conclusion that managers are right. They may not be. A better approach would be for consultants to gather information about organizational strengths and weaknesses and then see what common themes surface across many groups.

Before leaving this section, there is a third common scenario that consultants face. The situation is this: Managers call the consultants in but already have a solution in mind. When consultants ask about conducting an organizational assessment, they are assured by the managers that it will be a waste of time and money. It is a common problem in consulting. In addition, there are no easy, simple ways to cope with this problem. If consultants assume managers are correct and act accordingly, they are placing themselves at risk of applying the wrong solution because they have not checked the issues. They have failed to perform their due diligence. It would be akin to going to a doctor, asking for medicine, and then assuring the doctor that no diagnosis is needed because the patient already knows the cause.

1.5 Where Is Organizational Assessment Conducted, and How Does Context Affect the Assessment Process?

Carrying out a comprehensive or situational assessment is similar to conducting a research project. An assessment is research, though practitioners often become nervous when they hear that word because it evokes bearded professors exploring useless information about how many angels can dance on the head of a pin. But research provides important clues about the proper, and rigorous, ways to carry out a systematic investigation.

Any good research project follows several key steps:

1. Clarify the issue(s) to be investigated.
2. Gather information about the background of the issues to be investigated.
3. Refine the issue(s) to be investigated based on the results of step 2.
4. Specify the meaning of terms so they are clear and not liable to be misunderstood.
5. Decide who is to be the focus of the investigation.
6. Clarify and refine data collection methods.
7. Collect data.
8. Analyze the data.
9. Draw conclusions about the data.
10. Communicate the information to stakeholders.

Use the worksheet shown in Table 1.1 to help plan the organizational assessment based on these steps.

Step 1 means to clarify exactly what issues are to be investigated. If consulting clients are complaining about high turnover or low morale, then that presenting problem is sufficient as a starting point for writing a proposal.

Step 2 refers to the mini-scan. Consultants must gather information about the issue(s) and the setting(s). If employee engagement is the issue, then consultants should gather information about the organization and about engagement.

Step 3 means to revisit the initial issues based on the information gathered in step 2. Information gathered in step 2 may indicate new ideas to be investigated. They are reflected in this step and are discussed with clients to ensure they understand.

Step 4 centers on specifying the meaning of terms. The scientific method requires precision of language. Terms must be operationally defined.

Table 1.1 *A Worksheet for Planning Organizational Assessment Based on Research*

Directions: Use this worksheet to plan an OD assessment based on research. For each question posed in the left column, provide your answers in the right column.

	Questions Have you...	Your Answers for the Organizational Assessment Plan
1	Clarified the issue(s) to be investigated?	
2	Gathered information about the background of the issues to be investigated?	
3	Refined the issue(s) to be investigated based on the results of step 2?	
4	Specified the meaning of terms so they are clear and not liable to be misunderstood?	
5	Decided who is to be the focus of investigation?	
6	Clarified and refined data collection methods?	
7	Collected data?	
8	Analyzed the data?	
9	Drawn conclusions from the data?	
10	Communicated the information to stakeholders?	

Step 5 identifies the population, stakeholders, and any sample. The step addresses from whom information should be collected, and how many people will lead to fair conclusions backed by the data.

Step 6 focuses on how data will be collected about the problem, issue, or organizational strength. Typical data collection methods may include surveys, interviews, focus groups, observation, secondary data (such as information already existing in the organization's records), or some combination. Data that are triangulated (double-checked from multiple sources) is usually considered more useful than data collected unchecked from a single source.

In step 7, consultants must collect data. This step has to do with implementation of data collection methods. How data are collected can affect results.

In step 8, consultants analyze the data. They may use quantitative analysis (such as statistical methods), qualitative analysis (such as content analysis of words), or blended methods.

In step 9, consultants draw conclusions about the data. In OD, consultants rarely draw conclusions but instead, feedback common points of agreement and disagreement gathered from respondents to their data collection methods.

In step 10, consultants communicate information to stakeholders. How data are fed back is a strategic issue that influences stakeholder acceptance. For instance, if a survey is conducted and only senior leaders see results, workers may be suspicious about the survey results and any decisions made that stem from those results.

1.6 Why Is Organizational Assessment Conducted?

Any effort to assess the organization is a change effort in its own right. Collecting data raises expectations for change. If no change is made—or people do not receive feedback about the data collected—then they grow disenchanted (and potentially actively disengaged). So great care should be taken in deciding what to collect data about and how to phrase questions because they shape expectations.

Organization assessment is conducted to build awareness of organizational issues, pinpoint real issues (rather than symptoms) to be addressed. It can also help to build readiness for change by building expectations for it.

1.7 How Is Organizational Assessment Conducted?

OD can focus on surfacing and solving problems or on pinpointing and leveraging strengths. Assessment is needed for either purpose.

If OD is focused on leveraging organizational strengths, the need exists to identify what those strengths are. That can be done through positive story-telling with many stakeholder groups. For instance, ask questions like these to surface common strengths:

- Tell me a story about a time when you felt good about organization X?
- What happened step-by-step?
- Who was involved?
- When did this happen?
- Where did this happen?
- What was it about the situation that made you feel good?

Although one person's answers to these questions will not be that useful, the patterns that emerge across many interviews will help identify organizational strengths. Gathering that information can be assessment. Later, in an appreciative inquiry summit, organizational members can be put through storytelling centered on these areas of strength. That whole process is assessment.

1.8 How Is Organization Development Assessment Different from Other Consulting Approaches to Organizational Assessment?

OD consultants should remember that they should not play experts like medical doctors. If they do that, they are using a medical model that begins with data gathering about the symptoms, diagnosis to discover root causes that result in the signs and symptoms, and prescriptions for what should be done to address the root causes. That approach, when centered on human resource issues, is typical of performance consulting (Rothwell 2013).

But OD consultants function more like clinical psychologists. They are facilitators. They rarely, if ever, offer personal opinions. They should trust that the real experts in a business are already in the business, but that the real problem is that they do not share the same understanding of problems, the causes of those problems, the priorities for problems to be solved, the best solutions for those problems, action plans for implementing solutions, and metrics by which to measure success. The OD consultant's role is to serve as facilitator in this process, helping stakeholder groups reach some level of agreement. Assessing the issues and feeding them back is critical to helping people agree on problems, solutions, action plans, and results.

Bibliography

Harrison, M. 2004. *Diagnosing Organizations: Methods, Models, and processes.* 3rd ed. Thousand Oaks, CA: Sage Publications.

Howard, A., and Associates. 1996. *Diagnosis for Organizational Change: Methods and Models.* New York: The Guilford Press.

Levinson, H. 1976. *Organizational Diagnosis.* Cambridge, MA: Harvard University Press.

Lusthaus, C., Adrien, M., Anderson, G., Carden, F., and Montalvan, G. (Eds.). 2002. *Organizational Assessment: A Framework for Improving Performance.* Washington, DC: IDRC Books.

Levinson, H. 2013. *Organizational Assessment: A Step-by-Step Guide to Effective Consulting*. Washington, DC: American Psychological Association.

Rothwell, W. 2013. *Applying Performance Improvement in Human Resource Development*. New York: Wiley.

Weisbord, M. 1978. *Organizational Diagnosis: A Workbook of Theory and Practice*. New York: Basic Books.

Chapter 2

Diagnosing and Assessing Organization Development Effectiveness

Angela L.M. Stopper and Jennifer L. Myers

Contents

2.1 Introduction

Now that Chapter 1 has given you an introduction and overview of organizational assessment and diagnosis from a practitioners' view and has discussed some of the theory you will need in order to apply these learnings in your own organization, we want to officially start your learning journey. This chapter will discuss the methods for diagnosing and assessing organization development (OD) at organization-, group-, and individual levels. We will also explore how to evaluate effectiveness at each level. Central to this chapter are the ties between an organization's strategic plan and the alignment of talent strategy, structure, technology, culture, and external competitive market strategies.

It is without question that the ultimate key to successful organizational interventions is precise organizational diagnosis. Therefore, as an OD practitioner, you are responsible for providing expertise and assessment tools that assist leadership in quickly and accurately determining the climate and culture that currently exist within their organization. Assessing and diagnosing the organization is critical because it sets the framework for identifying the issues using valid and reliable data.

During your very first meeting with clients (be they internal or an external, contracted client), they will often come to the meeting with an idea of what the organizational problem is. In the business, this is called the presenting problem. It is the problem that the client can see and therefore is the problem he or she wants to fix. The issue is, often the presenting problem is simply a symptom of something bigger, and often harder to fix. So, if you hear in a meeting that your client knows what is wrong and has a plan on how to fix it, do not just take his or her word for it. As the neutral party, it is your responsibility to enter into the diagnosis and assessment with no preconceived ideas about what is needed. You must explore the issues, find the data, and determine if the initial problem is truly the problem, or simply a symptom of something else. This can be challenging at times; therefore, it is imperative that you keep an open mind and base your recommendations on the facts from the analysis of the data you have gathered.

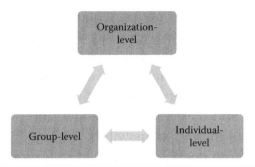

Figure 2.1   The organization-level, group-level, and individual-level strategies need to be aligned to achieve the strategic plan and goals of the organization.

Now, we will review the methods of assessment strategies that will guide you in your decision-making to achieve the desired outcomes for the stakeholders. But before we begin, let us just say one thing as it relates to level. To be most successful, the organization-level, group-level, and individual-level strategies need to be aligned to achieve the strategic plan and goals of the organization. The group level and the individual level should never be stand-alone levels because each level contributes to the overall success of the organization. See Figure 2.1 for a visual representation of this idea.

2.2 Assessment Strategy at the Organization Level

In an assessment completed at the organizational level, you will look at the entire function of the organization including: processes, people, behaviors, structures, technology, organization goals and strategic plans, compliance, the organization's customer base, climate, and culture. You will often need to review the organization's current state by observing the employees, leadership's interactions with the employees, new products or services being offered, products or services being considered as additions to the mix, and any changes being implemented. The key here is to gather data and analyze it in order for decisions to be made that will move the organization from the current to desired state.

To do so, start with a preliminary review of the organization with the goal of determining if the key stakeholders will cooperate and collaborate with you in determining the real issues or problems affecting the organization's performance. In this opening discussion, if it becomes clear that your client is looking for a quick fix within a specific short time frame, you may choose not to continue the discussion. Remember, OD is not a quick fix, it is not management consulting, and it is not prescriptive. It is a rigorous process that takes commitment and dedication, especially if you are working with a full organizational assessment with the goal of corporate culture change.

In your preliminary review, some of the diagnostic methods you can use are a review of documents, interviews, focus groups, survey data, customer and vender feedback, and observation of people, and processes during normal operations. Each of these options will be explored in greater detail in Chapter 6, when we more deeply discuss data collection.

If you have successfully completed your preliminary review and choose to proceed with the venture, your next step should be to develop a project scope. This often includes measurable, actionable goals, milestones with time frames, and a detailed communication plan. When creating the project score, be sure to consider details related to what, when, how, why, and where the diagnostic methods mentioned above will take place. Work with the organization to determine what communication tools it uses to spread the word of the progress of the initiative. Discuss how both you and they will reach out to the stakeholders, specific steps that will be taken, accountability parties for each step, and the expected benefits from each step and the overall OD engagement related to the entire organization.

Remember, key to successful OD is the need for those involved to give you honest information to accurately diagnose the organization. This can only be accomplished if you have appropriate access to the population being assessed and trust. Therefore, it is critical that you as a practitioner and consultant in this field can establish a rapport easily and that you are able to find and engage the appropriate organizational champions for each initiative you undertake. When finding an organizational contact and champion, it is critical that you identify someone (this can be multiple people) with access to both organizational leadership and to employees and that you work to build a solid relationship before the assessment and diagnosis formally begins.

You may be asking yourself, does the information you gather need to remain confidential and anonymous, or is it better for the organization to track who says what? It is important to answer this question prior to starting data collection. You should never assume that the data gathered from the employees will be kept confidential, and you need to clarify this point with your client. After it is clarified, it is critical that you inform those from whom the data is being gathered if it will be kept anonymous or not. As we have said, trust is the key in OD interventions, and you need to ensure honesty at all time, in order to build and maintain that trust. Never assume understanding. Never assume everyone is on the same page. Never get caught in what we call a lie of omission (when it is discovered that assumptions were made counter to your intention and you did not say anything to correct those assumptions). But regardless of whether information is kept confidential or not, you must ensure that any information employees give about the organization will not result in any repercussions in their performance reviews or their employment with the organization.

So, what should you look for when performing this level of assessment? Often, it is important to ask for current performance data, customer feedback, and employee surveys. If the organization's data is not current or valid, you will need to gather the data yourself. You then need to complete the diagnosis of all of your data, review the data provided by the organization, and compile the information into a clear and concise analysis using visuals. Steps to address this phase of the intervention are detailed in Chapter 7.

Remember, the goal of the diagnostic assessment is to identify the gap(s) between the current state and the desired state of the organization. Large-scale diagnoses and assessment of an organization must be structured and carefully planned with a timeframe of completion.

Remember the importance of communication in this process. In order for any approach to become operational, it is critical that it has been appropriately communicated to those who have a stake in the outcome, or those who are impacted by it.

2.3 Assessment Strategy at the Group Level

At the group level, you will often be contracted to complete an organizational assessment in departments, project teams, or any smaller part of the entire organization that works together to reach specific goals. To do so, you can review the group's processes, structure, and performance. In today's organizations, this can be challenging, as companies have employees from around the world working in virtual teams. A key step is to find out where the group members are located and build a plan to reach out to them where they are, as opposed to asking them to come to you. This can be done using technology, of course, but it is critical to ensure employees feel like you are making an effort to understand their performance in their work environment (not in a vacuum).

If those employees whom you need to reach are all working on-site at the organization, you can schedule face-to-face meetings. If the group is working across the world in different countries, you need to find out how its members are currently comfortable meeting and communicating, and build that knowledge into your data collection strategy. If you do choose to use technology to aid in your data collection, know that there are two main options, synchronous (at the same time) or asynchronous (at different times). In synchronous technology-aided communication, everyone meets in real time (think online meetings and tools like Adobe Connect and Skype). Synchronous meetings can be difficult to schedule because of time zones and regional holidays. In asynchronous technology-aided communication, group members can come to the meeting whenever they wish and add to the conversation (think discussion boards and the like). An important thing to keep in mind if you choose to use asynchronous technology-aided communication, be sure to set a firm start and stop time for each *discussion*. If not given these limits, individuals will often not participate because of the lack of time urgency. Keeping discussions open for a week, and at the longest two weeks, has been the best practice that we adhere to.

Some important questions to answer in reviewing a group-level processes, structure, and performance include the following:

- Is the group aware of their goals?
- Is the group meeting set goals in an agreed upon time frame?
- What are the interpersonal relationships within the group?
- Are the roles and responsibilities clear to each member of the group?
- Are the interdependencies of the roles and responsibilities clear to each member of the group?
- What are the gaps with the group's knowledge and skill level?
- Is the group sufficiently planning for future success?
- Do all members of the group understand the organization's goals, mission, vision, and strategic plan?
- Does the group's goals align with the organization's goals, mission, vision, and strategic plan?
- Do individuals in the group understand the role they play related to the organization's goals, mission, vision, and strategic plan?

To find the answers to these and other questions, you will often need to facilitate group meetings, observe the group's interactions, and outline group decision-making and problem-solving processes. Conversations at the group level as well as at the organizational level are needed in order to ensure proper strategic alignment.

2.4 Assessment Strategy at the Individual Level

When looking at assessment strategies at the individual level, it is important to first look at the individual's job description, work responsibilities, and past performance reviews. If possible, try to observe the individual's behavior during interactions with other employees and their supervisor during work hours.

It may also be important at the individual level to have hard and fast tools to help you assess actionable and measurable work outputs. This is different than assessing opinions and assumptions about an employee's performance. See Table 2.1 to deepen your understanding of the differences between the two.

Table 2.1 Differentiating Fact from Opinion

Assumptions and Opinions of Work Outputs	Why These May Not Be True	What to Measure Instead
Comes in before 8 a.m. and leaves after 5 p.m., he or she must be a hard worker.	We call this time-clock management. Just because someone is at his desk for nine hours does not mean he or she is producing impactful work.	Instead of using time-clock management, measure performance against agreed upon outputs and timelines.
Everyone likes the individual, so he or she must be a strong team player.	Being liked and being effective are two different things. Just because someone is the life-of-the-office, does not mean he or she is using his or her time and resources in the most impactful way.	Instead of using popularity, measure performance against agreed upon outputs and timelines.
Office gossip says that this person is a mess and his or her work is suffering.	Gossip happens for a number of reasons, none of which should make their way into an individual's assessment.	Instead of using the office grapevine, measure performance against agreed upon outputs and timelines.

So this is all well and good, but how do you ensure you are not using time-clock management, popularity, or the office grapevine in an individual-level assessment? You instead use one or a combination of the following tools:

- 360-Degree assessment
- 180-Degree assessment
- 90-Degree assessment
- Dossier (portfolio) assessment
- Simulations/assessment centers
- Performance tests

This list is not meant to be exhaustive and you should expect to mix and match the tools you need in order to achieve the results you desire. Often, one tool will not get you everything that you need. In order to properly combine the tools, let us take a minute to look at each of them in a bit of detail.

2.4.1 360-Degree Assessment

In a 360-degree assessment, individuals rate themselves on a list of criteria or competencies (as measured by behaviors or outputs), or work standards (as measured by preestablished work targets). The individual is then rated on the same criteria by those who work below them and for them (subordinates), with them (peers), and above them (managers), giving a full picture or 360-degree view, of the individual. The results reveal what individuals believe and what their raters believe about their level of competency or level of performance.

Generally, the results are delivered in a full report, including the score that the individual gave himself or herself, compared and contrasted with the averaged results from their rater group(s). This data can then be discussed with a coach, mentor, or OD practitioner trained in delivering the assessment in order to look for alignment, misalignment, blind spots and/or hidden strengths. The results are often deep and meaningful to employees who participate, and strong development plans can be built from the data, when properly collected and shared.

2.4.2 180-Degree Assessment

A 180-degree assessment resembles a 360-degree assessment, but the peer group is dropped. Raters comprise only those above and below the targeted individual on the organization chart. A major advantage of this approach is that it reduces the number of mathematical calculations to be performed when compared to a 360-degree assessment. A major disadvantage is that peers are sometimes the best judges of an individual's strengths and weaknesses.

2.4.3 90-Degree Assessment

In a 90-degree assessment, only two rater groups are used, the individual and his or her boss. This again simplifies the data gathering process, but severely limits the tool's impact by limiting the feedback to that of a person's boss.

2.4.4 Dossier (Portfolio) Assessment

Like in the art world, using the dossier approach in an organization allows individuals to showcase their work products as a sign of the competency in which they are able to successfully compete a job. For this type of assessment, individuals provide examples of their best work to raters, and the raters rely on a previously-prepared list of measurable quality criteria against which to render judgment. You can see how this can clearly give an OD practitioner a view into the skills and abilities of an individual. I am sure you can also see how time consuming this can be. Another consideration related to this form of assessment is bias. Individuals will obviously choose their best work, leaving out examples of times when they have performed at less than optimal. In addition, raters can be swayed if they know the individual being rated and are familiar with his or her general work outputs. That is why, in this form of individual assessment, it may be important to keep the identity of the person being rated secret (a blind review).

2.4.5 Simulations/Assessment Centers

In a simulation, those being assessed perform in a simulated setting, not a real work setting. The OD practitioner can then judge the person's success or failure, which can again outline developmental needs. Today, simulations and assessments can be performed in person or virtually. Every day, advancements are being made using game theory and virtual reality, producing new and interesting tools that practitioners can use to successful conduct this type of assessment.

2.4.6 Performance Tests

In a performance test, just like in any test, individuals are tasked to demonstrate what they know and what they can do. Using tools such as role play or group activities, OD practitioners can design tests that put individuals into situations where they need to demonstrate their knowledge and expertise. The key to using this form of individual assessment is a deep understanding of the desired performance behaviors and design creativity on the practitioner's part.

As with the two previously discussed levels, after analyzing the data you have gathered in an individual assessment, you must deliver the data back to the individual. You may choose to meet with the individual's supervisor prior to that meeting, or after. But a key thing to remember is that it is critical to have the supervisor's support as you outline the developmental strategies that come from any findings discovered in this type of assessment. Again, it is very important to define that communication process far before the assessment starts and to make sure everyone is aware of the process and the reasons it has been designed as it is.

Now that we have looked at some processes around OD assessment and diagnosis at different levels, let us take a step back and consider why it is important to ensure the link that we have said is critical. You will remember early in the chapter, we said: to be most successful, the organization-level, group-level, and individual-level strategies need to be aligned to achieve the strategic plan and goals of the organization. Thinking about that, please consider the following.

2.5 Vignette 1: Diagnosing with a Mission, Vision, and Strategic Plan

When beginning an OD assessment, it is critical to define the mission, vision, and strategic plan of the organization with the client and other engaged stakeholders. This will help guide your alignment of the assessment and diagnosis to the overall strategy of the organization. Only by doing this can you begin to see where the gaps are occurring and to narrow and prioritize the intervention or interventions that come from the process.

Let us look at a vignette where the client has a clearly defined mission, vision, and strategic plan.

Sung is a new manager, hired to lead the marketing team of a small public relation (PR) firm in the Silicon Valley. The company's client list is prestigious, but homogenous. They currently work with 30 clients, all in the same industry, all about the same size (employees and revenue), and all lead by very successful white, male chief executive officers (CEOs). His first task as a manager of this creative bunch is to set his team's goals. He begins by meeting with his boss, the head of strategy for the company, and learns that over the next three years, the company's strategic plan includes the following three main goals:

- Get out of print media
- Focus on social media marketing
- Revamp their client portfolio to include more diverse companies

With these goals in mind, Sung looks over his department's staffing, technology, and projects in progress. He immediately notices the following:

- His team is made up of four men, all Northern California natives.
- The office is cluttered with many back issues of print publications that the team has long been using as vehicles for their PR clients.

Sung decides to use his first pitch meeting as a vehicle to gather more data. He begins by asking his team to discuss their personal opinions on social media. To his surprise, no one on his team has a Twitter or LinkedIn account. Although they all have Facebook accounts, they all say they use it mostly to gossip and stay connected with friends, not *for business.*

Sung then asks each of his team to give him their target list, "Who are your big three companies to target for business in this next six months?" He notes the responses from his team, and after the meeting, moves to his office to do some quick research. He quickly notices that out of the 12 companies mentioned, 10 seem to fit exactly into the mold of current companies in the corporate client portfolio (about the same number of employees, all in the same industry, all in Northern California, all with white CEOs).

This is enough information for Sung to notice some gaps in the contribution of his team and the strategic goals of the organization. Sung is not sure where to start with aligning his department's goals to the organization's goals, but he knows something needs to change. Since he is a new manager, he does not want to appear ignorant on how to create departmental goals, but he also knows if he pushes his ideas regarding social media and client mix onto his team, there will be push-back. He quickly realizes that there is a need for cultural change in his department, and he calls his boss to discuss.

In review, the case scenario involving Sung is not uncommon for new employees, including managers. To be successful, Sung must make sure he is knowledgeable about the organization's strategic plan and goals as well as his team's understanding of their role in the big picture. He then needs to take the necessary steps to align his team with the organization's strategic plan or he faces potential disaster.

2.6 Vignette 2: Diagnosing without a Mission, Vision, and Strategic Plan

Let us now look at the same case, but without a clearly defined organizational mission, vision, and strategic plan.

Sung comes in on day one of his new job and meets with his boss. His boss tells him that it is goal-setting time, and Sung is expected to present his team's goals for the next year to the C-suite team in the next month. Being a smart manager, Sung knows the marketing team for the company is important to the overall success of the organization, and starts to do his research. Unfortunately, unlike our previous vignette, Sung is unable to clearly define the organizational strategy, so he begins like so many of us would in the same situation. He aligns his assessment and diagnosis on feedback from the organization's current product and service portfolios to see where the biggest successes are occurring and to see if there are any gaps that need to be addressed.

Sung meets with his team to get up to speed on what they are currently doing. He starts by asking for an analysis of their current client list to see who their biggest moneymakers are. He also asks the team to look over past hit rates with their hard copy publications and graphs where they are seeing the biggest impact for their clients.

Using benchmarking, Sung and his team determine a target list for new clients that closely matches those that have been most successful for them in the past. They also plan to increase usage of the current hard copy publications where they get the biggest return. Because the current marketing team is not terribly savvy with social media, they does not consider building a strategy around *those silly tools that the young people use to gossip.*

You can clearly see the different outcomes simply outlined in the above two stories. In both stories, Sung is not sure what goals need to be set for the team. In the second story, this uncertainty is compounded because he is not aware of where the company wants to go. Although the goals that are developed come from sound analysis and diagnosis, they do not show the need for the major change effort noted in the first story. This is a problem. Even though, in both stories, Sung knows how important marketing is to the organization's growth, the second story shows that he is unable to take the steps necessary for organizational success.

When a leader comes into an organization without a clear understanding of that organization's long-term strategic plan, and an understanding of how their team fits into that plan, he or she faces impediment of group effectiveness because it becomes impossible for the department and its employees to set goals to assist in the overall strategic achievement of the organization.

2.7 Understanding Your Role as a Practitioner and Consultant

In a way, you carry the weight of the world on your shoulders when you are assessing and diagnosing an organization and examining its overall effectiveness. It can be extra challenging for you to balance your responsibilities as an OD practitioner with the expectations of those leaders who think your job is to come into their organization and provide solutions to all of their problems. This, however, is not your role and it is important that OD clients understand this as early on as possible. Be clear and ensure your clients know the difference between OD and management consulting. Ensure they know your function and understand the expertise you, as an OD practitioner, can bring to their change efforts.

It is also tempting to listen only to what leadership and their executive officers tell you during the many meetings you will have during an OD effort. Again, leaders will have ideas about what they perceive as the problems that plague their organization. In some cases, they may be correct, but more generally they are only partially correct or not close to being correct at all. When you meet with leadership, remember why you are there. You are there to collect data and examine the organization through the OD assessment and diagnosis methods you have been so well trained in and experienced with. You are there to present the information in the most neutral way possible and, although at times leadership may not want to hear the feedback you have to share with them, this is the job you have been hired to do.

So, why may leadership disagree with your findings? Numerous reasons such as:

- C-suite bias
- A history of past success, blinding them to the needed change for future success
- Lower level leaders shielding them from the true state of the organization to look good

However, the only way to truly begin resolving organizational change issues is to accept the assessment and diagnosis for what it is, authentic and fact-based. Your job is to assist leadership in seeing the benefit of customizing interventions to best suit the needs of their organization. To do so, leadership will need to take the data you have collected and begin to identify and implement reasonable solutions that are realistic and sustainable for their organization based on the defined problems.

2.8 Determining Effectiveness

2.8.1 Organization Level

Some organizations will want to know the return on investment (ROI) for an OD intervention. As we stated in Chapter 1, OD is notoriously weak in measurement. The trend is to move away from ROI to focus on *Business Impact* (which takes measures from each quadrant of the Balanced Scorecard).

You can also work to estimate the value of the interventions in the short-term and the long-term in improving efficiency and productively. This is much easier to do if you have linked the initiative to measurable business impacts that align with the overall organizational strategy. Can you show how the change initiative improved employee engagement? Maybe not. But can you show that after an employee engagement change intervention, participation in the monthly employee gathering increased by 25%? Certainly! The same goes for turnover, stress-leave incidents, and most other OD interventions.

The key is to agree with the client on the actionable and measurable change he or she wants to see and work with them to engage solutions that move the needle.

2.8.2 Group Level

With measuring the effectiveness at the group level, you can facilitate discussions and planning with the group to plan how and when they will assess their effectiveness, and value of the group to the organization in achieving the projects and goals. You can also look to supervisors, coaches, and mentors to gather the impacts that they see.

2.8.3 *Individual Level*

At the individual level, measuring effectiveness often relies on the supervisor. He or she is generally tasked with assessing an employee's skills and competencies yearly, so the impact of any individual level intervention can generally be wrapped into those standard performance appraisals.

Discussions can and should include action-planning sessions, where development plans are crafted and agreed on by all engaged parties. Development plans need to include the following:

■ Actionable, measurable goals
■ Time frames
■ Milestones/checkpoints
■ Support/resources needed
■ Accountability partners
■ Contingency plans

The employee needs to be held accountable for achieving the goals and expectations agreed on within the stated time frame.

A final assessment that should be completed is that of you, the OD practitioner, and your effectiveness. Whether you are an internal or external consultant, you need to evaluate your performance. This can be done by surveys, requesting feedback, and/or doing self-assessments during and after all OD interventions. Questions to consider including when engaging in a self-assessment are as follows:

■ Did the engagement achieve the desired, agreed on change?
■ What would you have done differently?
■ What would you keep the same?
■ What worked well with this organization?

Look to the worksheet at the end of this chapter to begin to design your OD self-assessment tool.

Being open to this kind of feedback on yourself as a consultant will help you to keep learning and improving your expertise in diagnosis and assessing OD. This is why keeping accurate records on your clients, whether you are an internal consultant or an external consultant is very important. That way, you have a record of what worked, what did not work, and if the desired outcomes were achieved.

2.9 Chapter Summary

In this chapter, we looked at diagnosis and assessing OD effectiveness at three levels, the organization-, group-, and individual levels. We discussed why the group level and the individual level must be in alignment with the organization level, and discussed two quick stories to outline the importance of that. We ended by talking a bit about how effectiveness can be measured, and leave you with some internal questions that need to be answered by you, as the practitioner, after all OD interventions.

In all situations, you need to be professional and ethical in the decisions that you make and the findings that you share when diagnosing and assessing OD. In Chapters 3 and 4, you will learn more about the models that you can employ and how to use each, depending on the needs of the organization, and which model will be a best-match with the organizational culture.

2.10 Worksheet: Crafting a Strong Self-Assessment of Your OD Intervention

At the end of an internal or external OD engagement, it is critical to give yourself time to reflect on what went well and what could have gone better. Use the below worksheet to craft your own self-reflection exercise that will ensure that you continue to learn from each engagement you undertake.

Organization Assessment—The Planning Phase	
Ask Yourself, Did You...	*What Would Have Made This Step More Effective?*
Involve the right people in the project?	What groups came into the project after it started? Should they have been included from the start? Who was mad/confused during the project? Would involving them have provided benefit?
Clarify the desired goals and outcomes of the assessment?	Did new goals emerge as the initiative moved forward? Should they have been included from the start?
Agree on what and who will be assessed?	At any point did the scope of the project change? What questions could you have asked in initial discussions to dig out those issues?

(Continued)

Organization Assessment—The Planning Phase	
Choose the proper assessment method(s)?	Did the assessment method provide you with all of the information needed? What new methods were introduced to fill in data holes midproject?
Choose the proper data collection method(s)?	Did the data collection method provide you with all of the information needed? What new methods were introduced to fill in data holes midproject?
Choose the proper analysis and data reporting method?	What questions did the client ask after you reported your findings?

Organization Assessment—The Data Feedback Phase	
Ask Yourself, Did You…	*What Would Have Made This Step More Effective?*
Design a feedback strategy for determining who gets what information how and when?	What groups were left out of the feedback sessions that came in later for clarification? Should they have been included from the start?
Prepare the appropriate people on how to use the results?	What clarification was needed by groups who needed to understand and utilize the data? What harm (gossip, misinformation, and misunderstanding) came after data feedback sessions?
Identify and diffuse anxiety?	What was done to combat the harm? Could steps have been taken in the beginning to eliminate having to use these measures?
Connect the feedback to action-planning?	What feedback was left undiscussed during action planning? Was this data necessary to include in the feedback at all? If so, why was it left unaddressed?

Organization Assessment—The Action Planning Phase	
Ask Yourself, Did You…	*What Would Have Made This Step More Effective?*
Involve the right people?	Who did you have to call into the room later in order to lead the changes? How was the initial champion successful in carrying out the change effort?
Develop a process?	How did the evaluation and prioritization process change over the course of the initiative?

(Continued)

Organization Assessment—The Action Planning Phase	
Build a solid plan?	How did the focus of the change effort change? How did the level of the change effort change? How did the end-goal change over time? How did measurement of progress change over time?
Build in proper contingencies?	What forces ended up working for or against the desired change?
Build a clear plan?	What roles needed to be clarified over the life of the project? What project objectives needed to be clarified over the life of the project?

Bibliography

Barnfield, H. (Ed.). 2014. *FYI for Your Improvement: Competencies Development Guide* (6th ed.). Los Angeles, CA: Korn Ferry.

Golembiewski, R. T. 2005. *Ironies in Organizational Development* (2nd ed.). New York: Marcel Dekker, Inc.

Rothwell, W. J., Stopper, A. L. M., and Zaballero, A. G. 2015. Measuring and addressing talent gaps globally. *Global HRD, 32*(1505), 1–18.

Rupp, D. E., Gibbons, M., Baldwin, A. M., Snyder, L. A., Spain, S. M., Woo, S. E., Brummel, B. J., Sims, C. S., and Kim, M. 2006. An initial validation of developmental assessment centers as accurate assessments and effective training interventions. *The Psychologist-Manager Journal, 9*(2), 171–200.

Additional Online Resources

International Association of Human Resource Information Management: http://ihrm.org.

Organization Development Network: http://www.odnetwork.org.

Society for Human Resource Management: http://shrm.org.

Chapter 3

Diagnostic Models following Open Systems

Hyung Joon Yoon

Contents

3.1 Introduction

Organizational diagnosis involves data gathering and analysis with an aim to feed the collected data back to a client organization to initiate a change effort. Without a model, practitioners must rely on their hunch when identifying the data to collect. With a model, it becomes possible to collect and analyze data with a clear mechanism. A model involves key variables of an organization such as strategy, task, people, and process. Usually models have graphical representations, clearly depicting the relationships among organizational variables. Models allow organization development (OD) practitioners and clients to understand a complex issue in a simplistic manner.

Why do you need to learn about diagnostic models? First, diagnostic models help OD practitioners plan for and implement organizational assessment and feedback. Second, as organizations are complex with a number of variables, relying on effective models can be comparable to having a map in a maze. Third, skilled practitioners end up where developing a new, customized model is necessary for their diagnostic activities. Without knowing different models, it is almost impossible to develop a model that works effectively in practice. To summarize, learning about different diagnostic models will allow OD practitioners to perform effectively even without significant prior experience. As you gain more experience, you can also synthesize elements from different models and create a customized model that best suits a given context.

Using a diagnostic model is very helpful. However, it could lead you to not-so-effective results when you have no strong rationale behind choosing a certain model, given the unique context of the client organization. Remember that each model represents a unique perspective; the data collected will be limited to the framework of the model.

Many existing organizational diagnosis models are based on the so-called doctor-patient approach. As an OD professional, you need to reinterpret the models from an OD perspective. As described in Chapter 1, organizational diagnosis in an OD context requires you to empower your client to engage actively in change efforts even during the assessment and feedback phase.

Chapters 3 and 4 are devoted to diagnostic models. In this chapter, you will be exposed to different models based on open systems, which imply that organizations interact with the environment. Even if an OD practitioner wants to use a model in Chapter 4, such as a model for assessing organizational readiness, an open-systems model should accompany with the model to gain a better understanding of the organization. Because diagnostic methods are built upon a model, this chapter serves as a foundation for subsequent chapters on planning, gathering, and analyzing data.

3.2 Basics of Assessment and Diagnosis

The two main approaches to OD are as follows: (1) the problem based approach using the Action Research Model (ARM) and (2) the strengths-based approach using Appreciative Inquiry (AI), pursue different outcomes from assessment and diagnosis. Although the terms *assessment* and *diagnosis* could be used interchangeably in the case of ARM, *diagnosis* does not apply to AI due to a philosophical difference. When using AI, the primary interest is to identify the positive core of the organization (D1), desired future dreams collectively (D2), identifying ways to fill the gap between D1 and D2 (D3), and taking a collective action to fill the gap (D4) (see Figure 3.1).

In this chapter, we review different models that fit better with ARM. Keep in mind that the aim of diagnosis (assessment) in the context of ARM is to identify a gap between the current and desired states of an organization regardless of which model you choose (see Figure 3.2). When applying different models, use the models to understand both the current state and the desired state of the organization. Then, carefully compare the two states. This will help you generate directions, goals, and objectives for the intervention. Usually applying diagnostic models is about connecting the dots and ensuring the congruence among the elements within the models. While connecting the dots, OD practitioners find out where discrepancies exist and how alignment between the variables could be achieved.

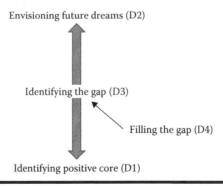

Figure 3.1 What to assess when using AI.

Figure 3.2   What to assess when using models relevant to ARM.

3.3 Overview of Open-Systems Models

Open-systems models assume that an organization does not exist in a vacuum. Historically, organizational theories have overlooked environmental influences on the organization, treating it as a closed system. Open-systems models, however, consider the interactions between internal organizational elements and the external environments. Also, open-systems models are cyclical, addressing input, transformation, and output (see Figure 3.3). The output becomes the input for the next cycle and transformation occurs in an organization to produce a new output while interacting with the environment.

Open-systems models have evolved from closed-systems models that lack input, output, and the environment. A representative closed-systems model is Leavitt's (1965) diamond model that defines such organizational variables as task, structure, technology, and the people represented in Figure 3.4. *Task* variables refer to expected activities that employees perform to deliver products and services. *Structure* variables refer to any structure that employees are supposed to follow. Examples include an organizational chart, hierarchical and horizontal communication, and work process. *Technology* variables refer to all tools, machines, and equipment that support employees' tasks. *People* variables refer to employees and key

Figure 3.3   Open-systems model.

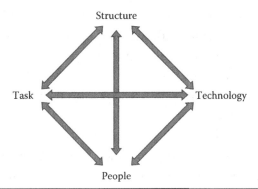

Figure 3.4 Leavitt's diamond model, a closed systems model. (Adapted from Leavitt, H. J., Applied organizational change in industry, in March, J. G. (Ed.) *Handbook of Organizations*, Chicago, Rand McNally. Copyright 1965 by Rand McNally. Reprinted with permission.)

stakeholders who carry out the organization's tasks. The arrows in the model indicate the nature of interdependence among the variables. If a new task is defined, an organization must find a suitable person for the task and provide tools to carry out the task (technology). Sometimes introducing a significant technology may prompt the organization to adjust its workflow (structure).

Leavitt's Model addresses internal elements of an organization in a most simplistic way by having four core elements and addressing the congruence among them. Would it be possible for you to transform Leavitt's Model to an open-systems model? Yes, it is possible. Then, how could it happen? Again, in a closed-systems model, there is a limited consideration of input, output, and the environment. If these elements are added to the Model, it could be turned into an open-systems model.

Before addressing open-systems models, let us review McKinsey's 7-S Model developed in the late 1970s by McKinsey & Co. This model is also considered a closed-systems model. Reviewing it is helpful to gain a further understanding about the transformation process of internal organizational variables.

The 7-S Model (Peters and Waterman 1982) examines the elements that give a holistic understanding of an organization, including the following:

- *Strategy*, a course of anticipated actions that allow an organization to achieve a competitive advantage.
- *Structure*, how tasks or chains of command are distributed.

- *Systems*, which support the structure's effective functioning (a performance management system allows management to ensure that outcomes are delivered in a quality manner).
- *Skills*, or the individual and institutional skills within the organization.
- *Style* (sometimes referred to as organizational culture), how work is done in the organization.
- *Staff*, the employees in the organization.
- *Shared values*, or what the organization is exerting to achieve. Shared values represent the essence of what the members in the organization believe.

Let's briefly compare Leavitt's Model and the 7-S Model. As shown in Table 3.1, most of the elements of the two models correspond to each other, although the 7-S Model further defined the elements of Leavitt's Model. Strategy in the 7-S Model is wider than the task in Leavitt's Model, although, in essence, strategies are turned into tasks. Both models involve the structure element, but the 7-S Model further specifies it with a hard structure (structure) and a soft structure (style). People in Leavitt's Model are broken down to staff and skill. A unique feature of the 7-S Model is the inclusion of shared values, which is a central component of the model. The 7-S Model also ensures the congruence among all the seven elements. The 7-S Model is developed from a doctor–patient mindset. OD practitioners must devise a way to use it as an OD diagnostic model, by fully empowering the members of a client organization in the assessment and feedback process.

Table 3.1 Comparison between Leavitt's Model and 7-S Model

Leavitt's Model	7-S Model
Structure	Structure and Style
Task	Strategy
Technology	Systems
People	Staff and Skill
	Shared values

3.4 Key Features of Open-Systems Models

Open-systems models have the following five key features: (1) environment, (2) input, (3) transformation, (4) output, and (5) feedback and congruence. Figure 3.5 depicts an open-systems model that addresses the five common features across different open-systems models, including Weisbord's (1976) Six-Box model, the Nadler–Tushman's (1980) Congruence Model, Tichy's (1982) Technical–Political–Cultural (TPC) Model, and Burke and Litwin's (1992) Model of Organizational Performance and Change, Harrison's (2004) Open-Systems Model, and Rothwell, Sullivan, Kim, Park, and Donahue's (2015) OD Effectiveness Model. Out of the five key features, you gain understanding of the transformation elements by reviewing early diagnostic models—Leavitt's Model and the 7S Model—from a closed-systems view. In the subsections below, each of the five features will be introduced while synthesizing existing models.

3.4.1 Environment

What makes open-systems models realistic compared to closed-systems models is its consideration of the constant interaction between the organization and the environment. An organization's constant adaptation to the constant change in the environment has become essential for survival. For example, Apple grasped the technological changes very well

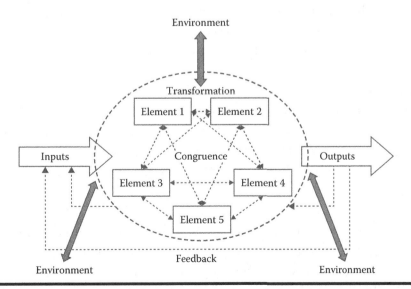

Figure 3.5   The flexible open-systems model: basic features of open-systems models.

and developed innovative products that influenced the environment. In turn, Apple's iPhone globally influenced its customers, potential customers, competitors, and suppliers. They were then challenged by their competitors, customers, and by legal authorities. This interaction between an organization and its environment continues.

For organizational assessment or diagnosis, considering environmental effects to the organization is critical, especially in determining the organization's strategic direction, which serves as input in an open system. The organization is affected by the environment, prompting it to develop a new strategy. A new strategic direction affects internal processes, structure, tasks, human resources, and so on. When a car maker attempts to launch a premium brand, it prompts the company to set up a whole new internal organization with new leaders with extensive experience in the premium market, resulting in changes in work process and culture. The environment can be approached with two axes: *level* and *aspect*.

There could be three levels of environmental analysis as follows:

■ *Micro*: This level represents the immediate environment with which one constantly interacts. It addresses an internal environment in an organization, including employees, workplace, policy, and financial status.
■ *Meso*: This level represents the near environment, which the organization can influence or be affected by. It could include customers, competitors, city policy, and associations to which the organization belongs.
■ *Macro*: This level represents the far environment, in which the organization can exercise no influence. It could include laws, technological trends, and demographic changes.

Environmental analysis could address different aspects of the environment. A popular term for the aspects is political, economic, social, and technological (PEST) analysis. Nowadays, environmental and legal aspects are also considered, and we use the acronym PESTEL analysis.

Then, how do you conduct a PESTEL analysis? The seven steps to do so follow:

■ Step 1: Identify the levels of analysis. In some cases, analyzing some levels is not necessary. For instance, if you are focusing on a team issue, the macrolevel analysis might not generate meaningful implications. Further, levels could simply involve near environment and far environment.

■ Step 2: Determine the aspects that you would like to use as lenses for analysis. The traditional PEST might work best for a certain context. Or, legal issues could be considered under the political aspect, depending on your context. If a certain environmental aspect is important, you could examine, for example, the demographic aspect more closely, instead of considering it in the social domain.

■ Step 3: Identify variables for information gathering. Table 3.2 illustrates variables that could be assessed, applying the three levels and PESTEL aspects. When considering your own environment, you must adjust, and further identify variables that are important to your context.

■ Step 4: Gather information about each of the variables defined. Search for information through the Internet and the library. Contact internal and external people who hold relevant information. Conduct interviews with them, record the responses, and request supporting documents.

■ Step 5: Analyze information gathered and describe relevant content from each section, for example, the political aspect at the mesolevel.

■ Step 6: Draw implications of environmental influences on the organization by examining information in each section.

■ Step 7: Prioritize potential impacts of environmental influences and generate ideas how the organization could manage them.

3.4.2 Input

Inputs could be resources, history, strategy, or mission, anything that helps organizations to shape outputs. According to Harrison (2004), inputs are any resources such as human, financial, material, and intangible resources supplied into the organization to produce outputs. In Harrison's model, input is identical to the resource. According to Nadler and Tushman (1980), inputs include environment, resources, and history. Nadler and Tushman consider strategy as an output of the inputs, which becomes an input for the transformation process. The environmental variable of Nadler and Tushman's (1980) model could be excluded from input, as the environment is a separate element in an open-systems model. Tichy 1982's Technical-Political-Cultural (TPC) Model does neither address input nor output; it rather emphasizes the environmental forces to the organization from technical, political, and cultural perspectives. Tichy, however, included mission and strategy as one of three core components of an organization with structure and human resource management. By taking Nader and Tushman's perspective, mission and strategy could be inputs.

Table 3.2 Examples of PESTEL Variables at Micro, Meso, and Macro Levels

	Micro	*Meso*	*Macro*
Political	Organizational hierarchy, power distribution, and HR policy	The power of the consumer group, alliance among competitors, industry-, or market-specific regulations	Government policy and regulations
Economic	Financial status of the organization, financial growth of the organization	The growth of the market, financial agreements, or norms with vendors and customers	Economic growth, exchange rates
Social	The culture and norms of the company, including interactions with its customers and suppliers	Relationships with customers and competitors	Demographic composition, aging, gender issues, and diversity
Technological	Internal R&D activities and adoption of technology	Specific technologies used in the market for commerce	Technological trends, automation, and use of machines
Environmental	Working conditions	Region-specific weather, climate change, or green movement	Climate change, weather
Legal			Labor law, environmental law, tax policy, health and safety law, and international trade law

There could be two steps to assessing inputs. The first step is to examine the resources of the organization, even without considering environmental influences. The resources could be the following:

■ Human resources
■ Financial resources
■ Physical resources such as manufacturing and office buildings
■ Material resources
■ Intangible resources such as the organization's history, culture, and competencies
■ Customer-base
■ Reputation in the market or society
■ Other resources

The next step is to identify a strategy based on the understanding of resources and environmental effects. While conducting organizational diagnosis, there could be two scenarios.

The first scenario is when the organization has a clear mission and strategy. There, it is just a matter of understanding them. However, the second scenario is when the organization does not have them. There, OD consultants must facilitate the organization to develop their mission and strategy. For that, the famous SWOT analysis could be very helpful.

SWOT represents strengths, weaknesses, opportunities, and threats. Strengths and weaknesses relate to internal resources, opportunities and threats relate to external forces. Internal elements (strengths and weaknesses) could include all resources of the organization. External elements (opportunities and threats, or environmental factors) can be identified through the PESTEL analysis.

There are two main cautions when conducting a SWOT analysis. First, practitioners conduct a SWOT analysis without setting an intended status, which could be a vision or a long-term direction of the organization. Without it, it is less effective when identifying SWOT elements. Second, practitioners often stop right after identifying the SWOT elements. This leads the analysis almost nowhere. Remember that a SWOT analysis develops strategies by considering all combinations of the internal and external elements, for example, strength–opportunity (SO), strength–threat (ST), weakness–opportunity (WO), and weakness–threat (WT). Once potential strategies are identified, the organization should prioritize them and select important strategies to adopt. See the template at the end of this chapter to help you perform a strong SWOT analysis.

3.4.3 Transformation

Transformation, also known as throughput, is common across closed- and open-systems models, but their sub-elements are different, depending on the purpose of each model:

■ Leavitt's Model (Leavitt 1965): As mentioned earlier, it focuses on four elements: *task, structure, technology*, and *people*. When using this model, examining the effects of one element on the other—for example, the effect of the new establishment of a R&D team on the HR strategy—must be examined, and efforts to make alignment across different variables should be made.

■ Six-Box Model (Weisbord 1976): This is one of the earliest open-systems models for organizational change with six elements, as the title indicates. They are: *purposes* (of the organization and consideration of organizational outputs), *structure, rewards, helpful mechanisms* (policies and procedures, information, equipment, technologies, and anything that can help fulfill the organizational purposes), *relationships* (among and between people and units, and between people and supporting mechanisms), and *leadership* (the competencies of leaders). In this model, leadership is viewed as an element that governs and monitors all other elements and their alignments.

■ Congruence Model (Nadler and Tushman 1980): Congruence among trans-formational elements—*task, individual, informal organization* (norms, culture, implicit procedures, and relationships), and *formal organizational arrangements* (procedures, policies, and physical work setting)—as well as congruence between the transformational elements, and elements in inputs (*environment, resources, history,* and *strategy*) are crucial in this model. Also, the model clearly depicts the feedback process from input to throughput, from throughput to output, and from output to input.

■ 7S Model (Peters and Waterman 1982): As described earlier, the 7S Model involves *strategy, structure* (of the organization), *systems, skills* (of employees), *style* (organizational culture), *staff,* and *shared values.*

■ TPC Model (Tichy 1982): Unlike other models, *technical* (formalized tools, resources, and policy), *political* (dynamics between the organization and the environment and within the organization), and *cultural* (collective beliefs and values of employees) aspects are considered for examining both environmental forces and internal elements of the organization. Through these three lenses, it examines the following organizational elements: *mission and strategy, organizational structure,* and *human resource management.*

■ Burke-Litwin Model (Burke and Litwin 1992): This model is called a causal model of organizational performance and change that considers both transactional and transformational elements of the organization. It addresses 12 variables, *external environment, mission and strategy, leadership, organizational culture, management practices, structure, systems* (policies and procedures), *work unit climate, task and individual skills, motivation, individual needs and values,* and *individual and organizational performance.* Excluding the environment and output factors, it has 10 variables for the transformation process delineating the interaction between individuals and the organization represented by leaders.

■ Diagnosing Individual and Group Behavior Model (Harrison 2004): This model addresses the effects of resources at the individual, group, and organizational levels. The internal elements at the organizational level include goals, culture, structure, technology, behavior, and process. The model assumes that they influence group level elements such as group composition, structure, technology, group behavior, processes, and culture. They, in turn, affect the individual elements including individual job, tasks, individual behavior, attitudes, and orientations. It is also assumed that all of these elements affect at individual, group, and organizational levels.

■ OD Effectiveness Model (Rothwell et al. 2015): This model incorporates the ARM and AI approaches while suggesting six steps to OD: inquiring, strategizing, planning, doing, revitalizing, and transformation. While following each of the steps, four internal elements—*strategy, process, structure,* and *people*—should be considered.

Table 3.3 summarizes and compares the internal elements of the aforementioned eight open-systems models with an aim to guide you through the process of selecting relevant variables for your context. Highlighted cells indicate that the elements in the same column overlap with other models. The structure and people elements are present in all open-systems models. Also, the systems (technology) element is in six out of eight models. Additionally, strategy, task, culture, and leadership elements

Table 3.3 Internal Elements of Open-Systems Models

Open-Systems Models	Internal Elements					
7S Model (Peters and Waterman 1982)	Structure	Systems	Staff	Strategy	Style; shared values	Skill
Leavitt's Model (Leavitt 1965)	Structure	Technology	People	Task		
OD Effectiveness Model (Rothwell et al. 2015)	Structure	Process	People	Strategy		
Harrison's Model (Harrison 2004)	Structure	Technology	Behavior	Processes	Culture	
Six-Box Model (Weisbord 1976)	Structure	Helpful mechanisms	Rewards	Leadership	Relationships	Purposes
Congruence Model (Nadler and Tushman 1980)	Formal organizational arrangements	Informal organization	Individual	Task		
TPC Model (Tichy 1982)	Structure	Mission/ Strategy	Human Resource Management			
Burke-Litwin Model (Burke and Litwin 1992)	Structure	Systems	Task and Individual Skills; Motivation; Individual Values	Mission / Strategy	Organizational Culture; Work Unit Climate	Leadership; Management Practices

exist in multiple models. There is no right or wrong answers for identifying internal elements for transformation; however, having the most common elements such as structure, people, and systems by default in a customized open-systems model is desirable. The choice of the rest of the elements is a matter of choice, given the philosophy and context of a client organization.

Now, as an OD practitioner, you should be able to choose desirable internal organizational elements for diagnosis in your setting and customize Figure 3.5 to be used as your framework, simply by placing your choices in the transformation section of the figure. Let's suppose that you have selected structure, systems, human resources, and organizational culture. What should be the next steps? First, you need to define the elements of your choice. Structure could mean organizational design and charts that indicate the chain of command and communication across the organization. How about systems? Systems could include a physical system like a performance appraisal system, but it also could mean written HR policies. If you want to assess only physical systems, using the word technology might fit better. However, the most important thing in the first step is to define it so that the meaning of each element is clear to everyone. Second, you will need to come up with data collection tools for each of the elements by creating or adopting questions. You could develop interview questions to examine the current and desired status of structure, system, and human resources. You could also employ a standardized assessment tool that measures organizational culture from different perspectives. The data could be triangulated by different data collection methods such as focus groups, interviews, and observations. Once you gather data, the next step is to find a gap by analyzing the data collected. After that, the results must be fed back to the client group to develop suitable actions to be taken. Examples of the synthesis of models and data collection tools using internal elements are presented in Sections 3.5 through 3.7.

3.4.4 Output

Outputs refer to products and services that an organization provides to its customers. Outputs, however, can include employees' well-being and satisfaction (Harrison 2004). Nadler and Tushman (1980) specified outputs at the following three levels: individual, group, and organization. At an organizational level, these three factors need to be considered: (1) goal achievement, usually determined by the organization's strategy, (2) resource utilization, which, from an economics point of view, is used to optimize scarce resources for maximum outputs, and (3) adaptability to the organization's changing environment. Nadler and Tushman considered group and individual levels as contributing forces to organizational outputs. If there is a logical link between specific group outputs and organizational outputs, the group outputs must be monitored. The yield rate of a production line will contribute to the achievement of the organization level goals. At the same token, at the individual level, if certain individual variables, for example, employee engagement and performance, could affect the organization's outputs in a positive way, the variables are desired outputs and should be tracked.

How can we assess outputs in an OD context for an organizational diagnosis? The needs of the organization regarding the intended change efforts should be determined. An OD consultant could pinpoint target output variables to monitor the progress and success of the change initiative. To gain more ideas about outputs, the balanced score card (BSC; Kaplan and Norton 2004) could be helpful as it specifies four domains of organizational strategies—financial, customer, internal process, and learning and growth perspectives. To make it relevant to output in an open-systems model, outputs from the financial perspective could include financial results such as profit, ROI, shareholder value, and revenue growth. Outputs from the customer perspective could include such variables as sales increase and customer retention rate. Outputs from the internal process perspective could include the lead time for responses to customers, the number of new products and services, and the progress of new technology adoption. Finally, outputs from the learning and growth perspective could include the increased level of organizational culture, leadership competency scores of leaders, and the participation rate of skill-building opportunities.

3.4.5 Feedback and Congruence

The beauty of open-systems models is the interaction among all levels—environment, input, transformation, and output—in a model. Feedback within an open-systems model is about how the organization actively uses information at different steps to improve variables. A newly developed system in the transformation process could be factored into input, resulting in an upgraded strategy. Another example is that the current poor output regarding customer satisfaction could be a threat for environmental analysis. OD consultants should know how a change in any step or area could prompt a change in different steps or area. To stay effective, an organization must be responsive and adaptable to changes.

Congruence could be understood as ensuring fitness across different levels and variables. There could be congruence between inputs and transformation variables, between transformation variables and outputs, and within the transformation variables. At the input level, if there is a mismatch between the environment and resources, the organization must revisit its resources to better cope with the environment. Likewise, at the transformation level, if there is a discrepancy between desired tasks and employee capacity, the organization must develop its employees' competencies.

Nadler and Tushman (1980, p. 46) developed potential matches at the transformation level, defined as follows:

■ Individual–organization
■ Individual–task
■ Individual–informal organization
■ Task–organization
■ Task–informal organization
■ Organization–informal organization

Likewise, to take the example of the TPC framework (Tichy 1982), it is crucial to examine the congruence among mission or strategy, structure, and human resources management, and to identify the desired and current state of the organization to develop goals for intervention. Remember these are just examples; if you identified customized variables in the transformation level, you will need to explore the congruence among your selected variables by carefully examining whether a certain change would require a change in a different variable.

3.5 Vignette of Synthesizing an Open-Systems Model

This vignette is about synthesizing the Burke-Litwin (1992) Model with the Six-Box Model (Weibord 1976). The Burke-Litwin model of an organization development and change involves 12 elements of an organization and depicts many interrelationships among the elements. This model is selected as it demonstrates that a change in any of the elements has consequences for several other elements. However, the Burke-Litwin model needs simplification as working with 12 elements and a multitude of relationships can cause confusion for the OD consultant and the client organization trying to use this model to make an accurate determination. The Weisbord Six-Box

Model has elements that are similar to the Burke-Litwin model but with only six elements, which remains comprehensive enough to capture the essence of an organization. The Six-Box Model, however, seems incomplete as the environment is the only output to the model.

The similarities of elements and the fact that both the Weisbord Model and the Burke-Litwin Model depict an open-system concept, make them a natural pair to be combined into a model that incorporates the best of both. The essential elements of both models are retained while incorporating the simplicity of Weisbord and the connections of Burke-Litwin. The elements in the transformation level of the new model are as follows:

■ Leadership: The leader is the one in the organization that sets the tone and direction for others in the organization. Often, the actions of this person are mimicked by the other members. This person will drive actions to completion to achieve the desired results. The leader may be in an appointed position at the top of the organization chart or someone from within the organization that may not be in an appointed position.
■ Structure: The organization alignment of resources, which when mobilized support achieving the desired results.
■ Vision: What our future would be, how are we getting there? The vision should be developed to support the goals of the organization and communicated vertically and horizontally throughout the organization.
■ Relationships: The central element used to secure cohesion between the elements of leadership, structure, and vision. Strong relationships result in these elements being connected and working together to establish a high level of performance. Weak relationships will be evident in poor performance.

Figure 3.6 shows a representation of this new model, combining the Weisbord and Burke-Litwin models.

For an example, using this model for an OD change, consider replacing a senior member of a management team such as a site vice president. Changes in leadership and vision are expected to shift the balance in the middle of the model. This will affect performance and possibly results if relationships becoming so strained that the existing structure becomes disconnected from the changing elements.

The simplicity of this model requires an understanding of what each element can represent. The application can be applied to a formal or an

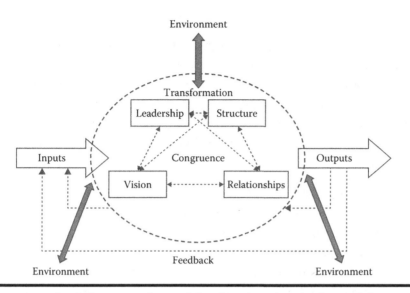

Figure 3.6 A synthesis between the Weisbord and Burke-Litwin models.

informal organization or in part. This application requires an open mind and adaptability to a situation. If it is desirable to have a model, which is very detailed and prescriptive to pinpointing trouble areas, this model would not be beneficial.

Although no model is perfect for every situation, there is no situation that would not benefit from using some model. The structure a model provides is a great reminder of key points to consider, and allows a consultant to become immediately immersed in a diagnosis effort. A model created by combining elements and key facets of several models shows a level of adaptability that is necessary when dealing with human systems in many situations. Keeping a model simple and relevant, like the combination discussed in this vignette, prevents us from getting bogged down in process, and allows the consultant the ability to observe more and worry about filling in less boxes.

3.6 Examples of Data Collection Tools and Results

The first example is interview questions used for organizational diagnosis in a small hotel, based on the Leavitt's Model. In this example, let's imagine that the OD consultant tried to address the key elements of the four elements. If you review the questions carefully, you will notice that the questions are mixed in current and future status, which was done intentionally to identify gaps.

Tasks:

■ What are the deliverables (services and products) your unit/team/department must provide? How do you deliver them?
■ How do your tasks affect the performance of the organization?
■ What would you like to change about your current tasks and duties?
■ Which kind of resources do you need to perform your assigned tasks? How do you get them? How would you like to get those resources?

Structure:

■ How do you operate within your unit/team/department? How do you communicate with them? What kind of changes are needed?
■ How is the organization structured? How would you describe an ideal hierarchy within your organization?
■ How are decisions made in your unit/team/department? In the organization? What impact do they have on the organization performance?
■ What kind of changes would you like to see in the decision-making process?

Technology:

■ Which type of machines and equipment do you need for your job? How necessary are they for your organization' performance?
■ Which equipment do you think needs to be changed or removed?
■ In what way do you think technology helps the organization and you? What about the future?

People/HR:

■ How would you describe the current arrangement of the human capital within your organization? What changes do you think are necessary for the future?
■ What kind of activities are conducted within your organization to enhance your performance, or improve the working conditions? What improvements do you think need to be implemented?
■ How do these actions influence your organization's performance?
■ What other factors affect the performance of you and the organization?

Let me provide a second example, where I summarize the data analysis results obtained by using the above questions (see Table 3.4). Data analysis results are categorized under current status and desired status, and in the column in the middle of the two, solutions to fill the gap were brainstormed. The owners and employees participated in the brainstorming

Table 3.4 Sample Data Analysis Results and Brainstormed Action Plans Based on the Leavitt's Model: A Vignette Discussing Analysis of a Small Moroccan Hotel

Constructs of Leavitt's Model	Current Status	Brainstormed Solutions to Fill the Gap	Desired Status
Tasks	• Trying to address customer satisfaction without clear guidelines • Supervising employees on a need basis • Owners are providing needed ingredients from Meknes	• Developing clear job descriptions is needed including the creation of new duties and tasks	• Waiters must know what are expected of them and act accordingly • One of the employees must supply ingredients to the kitchen
Structure	• Direct, face-to-face communications are happening • Has five workers without a clear chain of command • Most decisions are made after referring to owners	• Hire additional staff and train him/her • Promote a waiter to a supervisor position • Involve employees in decision-making	• Seamless service even during the high season • Limited needs for owners • Establish participatory approach in decision-making
Technology	• Usual material in Moroccan café (TV and WiFi) to attract customers • Owners and employees know of the importance of technology	• Purchase the needed materials	• Add a juice machine and an additional TV • Use pocket PC for ordering
People/HR	• Waiters benefit from accommodation, meals, and tips to motivate them • Stable productivity overall	• Develop training and team building programs • Establish reward programs	• Employees should be more engaged and work as a team • Highly motivated, self-directed workers who can respond to urgent needs
Congruence	• Waiters are not ready to use new technology • A lack of motivation system for employee engagement	• Need to train employees how to use new technologies • May need to develop a team-based compensation and benefit system	• Excellent congruence among all variables

session shortly after a feedback session. An OD consultant facilitated the sessions without imposing his viewpoints.

3.7 Example: A List of Documents That Could Be Gathered

During the data collection process for organizational diagnosis, gathering existing documents is necessary and crucial, as it can reduce unnecessary data collection and provide a holistic understanding based on factual data. The list below has been developed following the McKinsey's 7-S framework. As the elements in the 7-S Model cover most of the elements in different open-systems models, referring to this list of items will be helpful when requesting for documents to review.

Strategy:
■ Strategic plan
■ Overall firm-wide goals and budget targets
■ Cascading departmental goals that can be available via the organization's performance management system
■ Individual goal documents, which should match with the organizational strategy
■ Financial audit results

Structure:
■ Organizational chart
■ Business process/Procedural communications
■ Job descriptions
■ Customer satisfaction surveys

Systems:
■ Enterprise resource planning (ERP) systems used to inform the business/maintain compliance
■ Workflow diagrams
■ Interaction diagrams
■ Sampling of standard reports
■ Employee handbook
■ Standard operating procedures (SOP) for each relevant process
■ Technical design documents

Skills:
- Job descriptions
- Needs assessment or competency assessment results
- Previous training documents/assessments to determine existing skills
- Employee performance evaluation results
- Applicant aptitude testing/evaluations
- Talent management nine-box grid (High Potentials, low performance, etc.)

Style:
- Employment policies/handbook
- Satisfaction survey results
- Engagement survey data with focus on management activities/buy-in/ top leadership effectiveness
- Leadership training materials/introductory materials
- Management communications

Staff:
- Staffing metrics/demographics
- Succession plans
- Data on career paths
- Retention ratings
- Job/Position descriptions
- Organization design document
- Workforce plan

Shared Values:
- Mission, vision, and values statements
- Core competencies
- Information about business or employee resource groups (diversity and inclusion)
- Survey and interview result on shared values

3.8 Chapter Summary

Having a model for organizational diagnosis is like having a map in an unknown place. There are so many unknown variables in an organization, and a diagnostic model allows the OD consultant and the organization to identify the needs of the organization in a systematic way. Open-systems models are most common for organizational diagnosis in understanding how an organization works or should work.

An open-systems model has five key features such as environment, input, transformation, output, and feedback, and congruence. Understanding each feature and knowing how to assess the variables within each feature is necessary. This chapter proposed the flexible open-systems model developed for you to synthesize between different diagnostic models and devise your own customized model that fits with your client's context. Given practical examples of a data collection tool, a list of documents, and a synthesized model in this chapter, you are empowered to start your own diagnosis using your customized diagnostic model.

3.9 SWOT Analysis Template Tool

Practitioners can use the following tool to help compete an accurate and powerful SWOT analysis.

Vision/Mission:		
Internal ⟋ External	Strengths 1. 2. 3. 4.	Weaknesses 1. 2. 3. 4.
Opportunities 1. 2. 3. 4.	Strengths-Opportunities Strategies *Use strengths to take advantage of opportunities.* 1. 2. 3.	Weakness-Opportunities Strategies *Overcome weaknesses to take or by taking advantage of opportunities.* 1. 2. 3.
Threats 1. 2. 3. 4.	Strengths-Threats Strategies *Use strengths to avoid threats.* 1. 2. 3.	Weaknesses-Threats Strategies *Minimize or overcome weaknesses to avoid threats.* 1. 2. 3.

Bibliography

Burke, W. W., and Litwin, G. H. 1992. A causal model of organizational performance and change. *Journal of Management, 18*, 523–545. doi:10.1177/014920639201800306.

Dwyer, L., and Mellor, R. 1991. Organizational environment, new product process activities, and project outcomes. *Journal of Product Innovation Management, 8*(1), 39–48.

Farkas, M. G., and Hinchliffe, L. J. 2013. Library faculty and instructional assessment: Creating a culture of assessment through the high performance programming model of organizational transformation. *Collaborative Librarianship, 5*, 177–188.

Harrison, M. 2004. *Diagnosing Organizations: Methods, Models, and Processes (Applied Social Research Methods)* (3rd ed.). Thousand Oaks, CA: Sage.

Kaplan, R. S., and Norton, D. P. 2004. Measuring the strategic readiness of intangible assets. *Harvard Business Review, 82*(2), 52–63.

Leavitt, H. J. 1965. Applied organizational change in industry. In March, J. G. (Ed.), *Handbook of Organizations*. Chicago: Rand McNally.

Nadler, D. A., and Tushman, M. L. 1980. A model for diagnosing organizational behavior. *Organizational Dynamics, 9*(2), 35–51. doi:10.1016/0090-2616(80)90039-X.

Peters, T. J., and Waterman, R. H., Jr. 1982. In search of excellence: Lessons from America's best-run corporations. New York: Harper & Row.

Rothwell, W. J., Sullivan, R. L., Kim, T., Park, J. G., and Donahue, W. E. 2015. Change process and models. In W. J. Rothwell, J. M. Stavros, and R. L. Sullivan (Eds.), *Practicing organization development: Leading transformation and change* (4th ed., pp. 42–59). Hoboken, NJ: Wiley.

Rousseau, D. M. 1979. Assessment of technology in organizations: Closed versus open systems approaches. *The Academy of Management Review, 4*, 531–542. doi:10.2307/257853.

Tichy, N. 1982. The essentials of strategic change management. *Journal of Business Strategy, 3*(4), 55–67. doi:10.1108/eb038990.

Vadi, M., and Roots, H. 2004. The Estonian organizations-the subjects of transformation. Retrieved from http://discovery.ucl.ac.uk/17530/.

Weisbord, M. R. 1976. Organizational diagnosis: Six places to look for trouble with or without a theory. *Group & Organization Management, 1*, 430–447. doi:10.1177/105960117600100405.

Additional Online Resources

12MANAGE. (n.d.). Causal model of organizational performance and change (Burke and Litwin). Retrieved on January 2, 2016, from http://www.12manage.com/methods_burke_litwin_model.html.

Forklar mig lige. (n.d.). *Leavitt's Diamond.* Retrieved on January 6, 2016, from https://www.youtube.com/watch?v=DB0L5CAQgkE.

Jurevicius, O. (n.d.). PEST & PESTEL Analysis | Strategic Management Insight. Retrieved on January 6, 2016, from https://www.strategicmanagementinsight. com/tools/pest-pestel-analysis.html.

MindToolsVideos. (n.d.). The McKinsey 7S Framework: Learn how to align all parts of your organization's strategy. Retrieved on January 2, 2016, from https:// www.youtube.com/watch?v=7EqXqUDL47c.

Chapter 4

Diagnostic Models Addressing Environmental Forces and Organizational Readiness

Hyung Joon Yoon

Contents

4.1 Introduction

In Chapter 3, you learned about open systems models. In this chapter, we will discuss models that address environmental forces and organizational readiness. Assessing environmental forces for change allows organization development (OD) practitioners to develop strategies to implement change efforts by critically examining driving forces and restraining forces. Assessing the readiness of the organization is useful to determine organization development approaches that correspond to the developmental level of the organization. A synthesized use of different organizational diagnosis models will help OD practitioners to be insightful of organizational issues and OD approaches undertaken.

Understanding the environmental forces and the readiness of the organization helps OD practitioners to develop strategies to transform organizations. In addition, using a diagnostic model that aims to identify the positive aspects of the organization can be crucial for organizations that are ready for change. While Chapter 3 addresses models that can be applied to any organization, this chapter prepares OD practitioners to cope with the organization-specific variables of environment and readiness for change. The unitization of contents in the subsequent chapters depends highly upon the use of models addressed in this chapter.

4.2 The Importance of Considering Environmental Forces and Organizational Readiness for Change

As stated in Chapter 3, organizations do not exist in a vacuum, and the need for a change effort is often to cope with environmental effects. For example, recently, a major computer operating system (OS) company announced that they will no longer support the updates of an older version of the OS. However, many companies are still using the OS. If they do not upgrade it to a newer version of the OS, their computers will be vulnerable to security issues. Let's suppose that a company in this situation decides to purchase a new OS. The members of the organization must learn how to use the OS, and the company may need to upgrade other software programs that are no longer compatible with the new OS. This small environmental change prompts the organization to spend more money, schedule training programs, and face resistance to the change within the organization. In this situation, the force field analysis would be an excellent diagnostic tool to allow one to quickly develop strategies by considering different environmental forces.

Now, let's suppose that you are hired as an OD consultant for a company with 200 employees to shift the main focus of business from a wholesale distributor to direct sales through franchising. This transformative change requires a high level of employee engagement and strong buy-in from the top. Other than using an open systems model, what do you need to consider when conducting organizational diagnosis? One of the critical aspects is the organization's readiness for participatory change. What if the organization's leadership is very authoritarian, not allowing employees to speak up? What if there is good intention for employee empowerment, but there is no mechanism that can support the intention? If top management is not willing to make the change effort participatory, then it directly conflicts with the OD philosophy, which is highly likely to result in a failure.

One competency that all OD practitioners must have is the ability to know how to select the right client. Without an assessment that examines the organization's readiness for change, it could be detrimental for both the consultant and organization. Once you discover the level of readiness for change, you can strategize your approach for change.

4.3 Force Field Analysis

Kurt Lewin (1951) developed the Force Field Analysis to diagnose organizations in the change context (see Figure 4.1). Using Force Field Analysis, it becomes easier to understand what prompts the need for change by identifying driving forces and restraining forces for a current state. Also, by comparing driving forces and restraining forces, you can get an idea to what extent a change initiative would be challenged. The desired

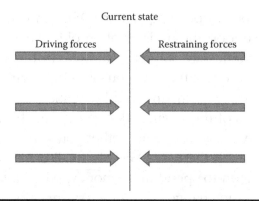

Figure 4.1   Force Field Analysis.

outcome of the Force Field Analysis is to develop goals to control the driving or restraining forces for a successful change initiative.

You can conduct a force field analysis by following the steps below:

1. Clearly define the current state, as it serves as a target for the analysis.
2. Examine the driving forces and the restraining forces for the current state.
3. Compare the two forces, prioritize their impact, and develop a goal after this analysis. It is helpful for you to rate each of the forces employing a 10-point Likert scale.
4. Driving forces can be strengthened by setting subgoals that maintain or intensify them. Likewise, restraining forces can be avoided by making up for them. Restraining force, for example, lack of communication could be addressed by a goal of the use of web-based conferencing system.
5. Once goals are identified, the final step is to develop strategies that minimize restraining forces and increase driving forces.

Force Field Analysis is a very simple but powerful tool for generating directions to manage a change effort. It works well when there is a specific issue for change. Remember that OD practitioners are in the position of facilitating the process of analysis including data gathering, reaching a consensus, and developing strategies through the involvement of the members of the client group.

4.4 Vignette: A Look at Force Field Analysis

4.4.1 Situation

A chief operating officer (COO) of WindGen asked Ron, chief human resources officer (CHRO), to increase their adoption of an enterprise-wide project management tool, ProM, to communicate to their leadership about financial forecasts and project health. For all departments in WindGen, visibility to financial forecasts is imperative for setting budgets and guidance for upcoming quarters and the next fiscal year. Visibility to project health is imperative for managing project delivery and any stumbling blocks to meet customer expectations and satisfaction. Ron called in an OD consultant, Cathy, and asked her to guide WindGen through the change process.

Cathy facilitated a focus group with five key stakeholders in the organization including the COO, CHRO, a project manager for ProM, and two other senior leaders. Cathy asked the participants to generate driving and restraining forces and give ratings for each of the items using a 10-point Likert scale. Her ratings are listed in Section 4.4.2.

4.4.2 Driving Forces and Impact Ratings out of 10

- Financial forecasting must be visible and accurate in order to properly set budgets and guidance for upcoming quarters and next fiscal year (*Impact = 10*).
- Visibility to project health and process is essential to ensuring on-time delivery of products and customer satisfaction by identifying and mitigating potential delays or stumbling blocks (*Impact = 10*).
- Use of the project management tool has been included in employee key performance indicators (*Impact = 8*).
- *Restraining forces and impact ratings out of 10.*
- Employees do not know how to use the project management tool (*Impact = 5*).
- The current state of the project management tool does not support their needs (*Impact = 8*).
- Employees joining the organization from acquisitions feel that how they track and manage information are better (*Impact = 3*).
- Employees do not know how to properly forecast financial information and document project progress (*Impact = 8*).

4.4.3 Ideas for Weakening the Restraining Forces

Cathy asked the participants to carefully examine the driving and restraining forces and discuss whether increasing driving forces would be helpful to the success of the project. The participants' answer was that the driving forces are already strong and it does not require close management. Therefore, they are asked to develop goals for weakening the restraining forces. For each of the restraining forces above, the following ideas were developed through a facilitated brainstorming process:

- Creating a training program to educate the employees on how to use the project management tool.
- Working with end users to collect an understanding of how the project management tool should be built to support their needs, generate requirements, and a release plan to improve the tool's capabilities.
- Developing an employee onboarding program within the human resources department.
- Creating a training program to educate the employees on how to properly forecast financial information and document project progress.

4.4.4 Strategy

Cathy further asked the focus group participants to develop an overall strategy for the change initiative by considering the above ideas. The overall strategy that bubbled to the surface of the discussion was to fine-tune the current version of the project management tool while training employees on how to use the tool and understand background information such as financial forecasting. An associated strategy was to monitor the company's budget plan, so purchases were made and training programs were delivered on time.

4.5 Practical Guidelines for Models Addressing the Readiness of an Organization

4.5.1 Likert's System 1–4

Rensis Likert is a widely known figure in the social science field. He is best known for the Likert scale. However, in the later stages of his career, he dedicated himself to organizational management and consulting. If you are interested in the life of this legendary figure, see Kish (1982).

Likert's System 1–4 Model is the outcome of his pursuits in the organizational domain and differs from the other models that we have reviewed so far. Instead of looking at different dimensions in the organization from an open systems' perspective, this model addresses an organization's readiness using Systems 1 through 4. The ultimate goal of an organization is to reach System 4.

In his book, *The Human Organization: Its Management and Value*, Likert defined the four main styles of leadership as follows (adapted from Likert 1967):

- In *System 1 (exploitive authoritative)*, management forces employees to follow decisions and generates fear to get employees to work.
- In *System 2 (benevolent authoritative)*, management provides rewards for work done, but the employees do not assume responsibility or exhibit teamwork.
- In *System 3 (consultative)*, management pays attention to some employees' ideas and provides consultation on issues raised, but there is a lack of responsibility among employees.
- In *System 4 (participative)*, management engages and empowers employees to solve problems using teamwork, and members in the organization share the responsibility to achieve the organization's goals.

Likert's model could be used during an organization development initiative to see the extent to which management is ready for a participatory change and to plan for a transformation from a lower level of participation to a higher level.

4.5.2 High Performance Programming Model

Nelson and Burns (1984) created a model called the High Performance Programming Model, which allows OD practitioners to identify (based on various levels) an organization's progress toward a high performance. Table 4.1 indicates the stages and areas within each level (adapted from Farkas and Hinchliffe 2013, p. 176). To determine an organization's level, OD practitioners can create a survey instrument or an interview protocol.

The original authors suggest using a 5-point Likert scale (5 = strongly agree; 1 = strongly disagree) to assess the following 11 areas (adapted from Nelson and Burns 1984):

- Time frame (past, present, future, and flow)
- Focus (diffused, output, results, and excellence)

Table 4.1 The Four Levels of the High Performance Programming Model

Area \ Level	Level 1: Reactive	Level 2: Responsive	Level 3: Proactive	Level 4: High Performing
Organizational focus	Reaction to urgency or threats	Short-term goals, incremental change	Active goal setting, planning, and commitment	Programming an ideal future, a superior sense of ownership
Locus of control	External	External	Internal	Internal
Organizational structure	Hierarchical, but ill-structured	Hierarchical	Flat	Flat with empowered structures
Management and leadership focus	Oriented toward Theory X, authoritarian, and enforces policies	Engaged in developing and coaching employees to solve problems	Engages employees in creating and achieving a shared purpose	Empowers employees to be fully self-directive and commit themselves to the company's goals voluntarily
Employee focus	Protection of themselves	Meeting the short-term goals or expectations	Organizational goals and responsibilities	A shared direction and a respect toward organizational culture
Communication within the organization	Disjointed and vague	Management sends a message to employees	Employees may provide feedback to management	Vigorous, using two-way communications at every level

- Planning (justification, activity, strategy, and evolution)
- Change mode (punitive, adaptive, planned, and programmed)
- Management (fix blame, coordination, alignment, and navigation)
- Structure (fragmented, hierarchy, matrix, and networks)
- Perspective (self, team, organization, and culture)
- Motivation (avoid pain, rewards, contribution, and actualization)
- Development (survival, cohesion, attunement, and transformation)
- Communication (force feed, feedback, feed forward, and feed through) and
- Leadership (enforcing, coaching, purposing, and empowering)

The results should be fed back to the client group and a sponsor, so they can see where they are and create a goal to move to a higher level.

4.5.2.1 An Example Using the High Performance Programming Model

An OD consultant tried to examine where her client organization fell between Level 1 and Level 4. For that, she took a look at and gave a rating for each of the elements in the high-performance programming model. Her conclusion was that the client organization falls within the Levels of 1 and 2, with seldom attempts at Level 3, as shown in Table 4.2.

4.5.3 The Great Place to Work Model for Highly Ready Organizations

The Great Place to Work Model is the most actively used model these days, which is applied in organizations over 40 countries and in major media outlets. The Great Place to Work Institute annually conducts extensive research using the Trust Index© Employee Survey and publishes the results, honoring the winners who exhibit an excellent level of credibility, fairness, respect, pride, and camaraderie. "A great workplace is one where people trust the people they work for, take pride in what they do, and enjoy the people they work with" (Burchell and Robin 2011, p. 1).

The model examines the following dimensions (adapted from Burchell and Robin 2011):

- *Trust*: Trust involves credibility, respect, and fairness.
- *Credibility*: Credibility is achieved through open communication, competence, and integrity.

Table 4.2 Illustration of an Assessment Applying the High-Performance Programming Model

High Performance Programming Model	Ratings			
	Level 1: Reactive	*Level 2: Responsive*	*Level 3: Proactive*	*Level 4: High Performing*
Organizational Focus	*Reaction to urgency or threats*	*Short-term goals, incremental change*	*Active goal setting, planning, and commitment*	*Programming an ideal future, a superior sense of ownership*
			X	
Rating Comment	The organization recently has decided to implement a performance management system that is integrated with talent management. This allows each department to align goals with the company's overall mission and strategy while tracking individual development plan (IDP). This is an indication that the organization is proactive and working toward high performance.			
Locus of Control	*External*	*External*	*Internal*	*Internal*
			X	
Rating Comment	The new performance management system has allowed leaders in the organization to be more proactive and responsible for the organizational goals and employee development. Although the system is newly introduced, it is already at 70% compliance.			
Organizational Structure	*Hierarchical, but ill-structured*	*Hierarchical*	*Flat*	*Flat with empowered structures*
		X		
Rating Comment	The structure is hierarchical with more than 50% of employees who worked for the organization more than 10 years. Because of the nature of the business closely tied to law enforcement, it seems to be inevitable to stay in a hierarchical structure.			

(Continued)

Table 4.2 (Continued)   Illustration of an Assessment Applying the High-Performance Programming Model

High Performance Programming Model	Ratings			
	Level 1: Reactive	*Level 2: Responsive*	*Level 3: Proactive*	*Level 4: High Performing*
Management and Leadership Focus	*Oriented toward Theory X, authoritarian, and enforces policies* **X**	*Engaged in developing and coaching employees to solve problems*	*Engages employees in creating and achieving a shared purpose*	*Empowers employees to be fully self-directive and commit themselves to the company's goals voluntarily*
Rating Comment	Employees are micromanaged, and they have to seek permission before acting in many cases. Employees often feel that their contributions are not valued. Employees feel limited in their influence within the organization.			
Employee Focus	*Protection of themselves* **X**	*Meeting the short-term goals or expectations*	*Organizational goals and responsibilities*	*A shared direction and a respect toward organizational culture*
Rating Comment	When the organization is financially challenged, the first thing that they do is to reduce headcount where necessary. Although the organization is financially secure, employees often feel insecure, resulting in protective behaviors.			
Communication with the Organization	*Disjointed and vague*	*Management sends a message to employees* **X**	*Employees may provide feedback to management*	*Vigorous, using two-way communications at every level*
Rating Comment	Supervisors receive messages and orders from senior leaders. They, in turn, repeat the same message to front-line employees. As they are relatively new to a supervisory role, their messages tend to be cold and lack a sense of connection with them. Although employees agree that management communicates clearly, they feel that a more two-way communication is needed.			

- *Respect*: Respect is reached through support, collaboration, and caring.
- *Fairness*: Fairness is achieved through equity, impartiality, and justice.
- *Pride*: Pride can be found in personal achievement, team performance, and the company's status in the community.
- *Camaraderie*: Camaraderie is built by facilitating intimacy, hospitality, and a sense of community in the workplace.

In this model, an organization's greatness is measured using the Trust Index, an employee survey, and a culture audit.

A great place to work with high levels of trust, credibility, respect, fairness, pride, and camaraderie is highly likely to exhibit the characteristics of Level 4 of both Likert's System 1–4 Model and the High-Performance Programming Model. As for organizational culture and the organization's readiness for change, the aim of the organization would be to make it Level 4 with the characteristics of a great place to work.

4.5.3.1 An Example Using the Great Place to Work Model

If your organization could afford using the Trust Index and the culture audit, you can gain quantitative results depicting the status of the organization compared to other organizations from the perspective of the six elements. However, even if you do not purchase the services from the Great Place to Work Institute, you can examine the level of your organization within the stated elements, you would just have a much harder time directly comparing your organization with the results of others.

Let's assume an OD consultant attempted to apply the Great Place to Work Model for her client organization without using the Trust Index and the culture audit. As a first step, she tries to see the developmental levels for the six Great Place to Work elements, while applying the Likert's System 1–4 Model, and converting it to a scale. Ratings are entered based on observations and interviews with employees, and rationales for the ratings are provided in Table 4.3. Because she is working with a large organization, she found it was also crucial to rely on a survey.

4.5.4 How Could an Organization Move from Level 1 to Level 4?

You have learned about different characteristics of an organization in terms of maturity and readiness for change through the lens of Likert's System 1–4 Model and the High-Performance Programming Model. Now the

Table 4.3   Illustration of an Assessment Applying the Great Place to Work Model

		Ratings			
		Likert Assessment Scale			
Great Place to Work Elements		System 1 Exploitive Authoritative	System 2 Benevolent Authoritative	System 3 Consultative	System 4 Participative
Trust	Involves credibility, respect, and fairness	*Management forces employees to follow decisions and generates fear to get employees to work*	*Management provides rewards for work done, but the employees do not assume responsibility or exhibit teamwork*	*Management pays attention to some employees' ideas and provides consultation on issues raised, but there is a lack of responsibility among employees*	*Management engages and empowers employees to solve problems using teamwork, and members in the organization share the responsibility to achieve the organization's goals*
			X		
Rating Comments		Most supervisors are relatively new to the company and their supervisory roles, and top management exhibits a direct, one-way communication to them. There are a set of rules to follow, and employees feel that they are constantly monitored by their supervisors. They do not feel motivated to take initiatives as they do not feel valued in the company. In addition, some newly hired employees left the company because of workplace harassment issues.			
Ideas for Future Directions		Revisit how messages are delivered from top to bottom. The roles and responsibilities of supervisors may need to be reviewed and restructured, if necessary.			

(Continued)

Table 4.3 (*Continued*) Illustration of an Assessment Applying the Great Place to Work Model

Great Place to Work Elements		Ratings — Likert Assessment Scale			
		System 1 Exploitive Authoritative	System 2 Benevolent Authoritative	System 3 Consultative	System 4 Participative
Credibility	Achieved through open communication, competence, and integrity.			X	
Rating Comments		The company implements a yearly job satisfaction survey with a response rate of 80%. The process of receiving answers from employees is nonthreatening and encouraging. Senior leaders debrief the survey results in retreats and ask for suggestions for improvement. Employees feel that their voices are heard. However, there has been a limited follow-up on the suggestions.			
Ideas for Future Directions		Engage all employees in the survey and create multiple implementation teams that will follow up on the identified issues. Written communication should also be encouraged to ensure everyone gets the same message.			
Respect	Reached through support, collaboration, and caring.		X		
Rating Comments		Because of a very high performance-oriented culture with a strict hierarchy, employees feel that leaders do not value collaboration and communication. Monetary rewards are in place based on metrics. However, nonmonetary rewards are scarce. Also, leaders are highly concerned of immediate performance, not long-term development of employees.			

(Continued)

Table 4.3 (*Continued*) Illustration of an Assessment Applying the Great Place to Work Model

Great Place to Work Elements		Ratings			
		Likert Assessment Scale			
		System 1 Exploitive Authoritative	*System 2 Benevolent Authoritative*	*System 3 Consultative*	*System 4 Participative*
Ideas for Future Directions		Utilize a set of core competencies that the company recently identified to guide the company's culture and behaviors of leaders and employees. Integrate cultural and developmental aspects in the metrics that the company monitors.			
Fairness	Achieved through equity, impartiality, and justice.	X			
Rating Comments		Front-line supervisors and employees both feel that there is a lack of fairness within the organization. There are rules and policies in place, but they are applied in a flexible manner by management, which results in intense feelings of inequality including gender issues. There are no clear guidelines for promotion. High performers sometimes feel left out because they are not promoted.			
Ideas for Future Directions		Identify inequality issues and their causes, and report the results back to top management. As a follow-up, HR policies and procedures need to be revisited.			
Pride	Can be found in personal achievement, team performance, and the company's status in the community.				X

(Continued)

Table 4.3 (*Continued*) Illustration of an Assessment Applying the Great Place to Work Model

Great Place to Work Elements		Ratings			
		Likert Assessment Scale			
		System 1 Exploitive Authoritative	System 2 Benevolent Authoritative	System 3 Consultative	System 4 Participative
Rating Comments		The company holds philanthropic events inviting survivors and their family. In the events, stories of the survivors are shared and they show gratitude to the company. Employees see how their work has major impacts on people's lives due to what they produce and become extremely motivated to work for the company.			
Ideas for Future Directions		Keep the practice and emphasize more on why the company exists. This can be a starting point for all other change efforts.			
Camaraderie	Built by facilitating intimacy, hospitality, and a sense of community in the workplace.	X			
Rating Comments		There is a lack of teamwork. Employees tend to care about their own performance and are used to follow directions from their supervisors. Even when other colleagues seem to be in need of support, employees do not often go beyond their job descriptions to help each other.			
Ideas for Future Directions		Supervisor need to encourage teamwork and improve working conditions by providing support and resources. Because of a highly performance-driven culture, it may be necessary to include collaboration in the individual performance metrics.			

question for OD practitioners is how to use the assessment results for future action. What should the organization do, if it is in Level 1 or Level 2? A list of eight steps that have been collected from 17 HR/OD professionals and synthesized in a sequential manner is as follows:

Step 1. A go-or-no-go decision
Some organizations and their employees might be satisfied with being at Level 1 or Level 2 without feeling the need for change. There a change effort is not required.

Step 2. Top management buy-in and willingness for leadership development
Without top management's buy-in, any change effort will fail. Because the transformation from Level 1/2 to Level 4 involves a great deal of time, resource, and dedication, top management should be committed to the change direction and willing to develop themselves further, as the Level 4 status needs a completely different style of leadership.

Step 3. Establishing a level of trust between management and employees
Without management trusting that employees can be involved in important tasks and decision making, next steps will not be achieved. Top management first must believe in employees' capability of leading the organization. Once management shows trust for the employees, they are likely to demonstrate the level of trust with the management and among the employees.

Step 4. Setting and communicating clear goals for change
Once management makes a commitment to organizational change and trusts their employees, they need to set clear goals for change, ideally using a participatory OD approach. If the employees participate in the goal-setting process, the need for communication is addressed during the process. If a top–down approach is used, the change goals must be actively shared and the organization needs buy in from its employees.

Step 5. Facilitate employee participation
Once clear goals for change are set, the organization must facilitate employee participation in every step of the change effort. Organizations should nurture the environment where employees can develop creative solutions. Employees and management must gradually feel their internal locus of control by observing the changes happening because of their efforts.

Step 6. Examining key elements in an open systems model
Once employees start actively participating in a change effort, the organization with its employees needs to examine key elements in an open systems model. As discussed in Chapter 3, assessment on elements

such as strategy, task, structure, technology, human resources, and culture should be carried out. Identifying positive aspects of the organization is also very important, as the organizational change could be built upon its positivity.

Step 7. Creating a environment for the best part of the employees
As much as leadership development is important for the capacity building of the management, it is also crucial to develop and engage its employees. The organization must nurture a positive environment where employees exhibit their best through cultural change, training and development, growth opportunities, better equipment, technology, and so on.

Step 8. Monitoring its progress through assessment and feedback
Through periodic organizational assessment, employee satisfaction surveys and organizational culture surveys, organizations can keep track of their progress and set goals for the next year. Other areas for change could be assessed periodically via both qualitative and quantitative assessments. The results of the assessments must be fed back to the members of the organization so they can act on them. Step 8 is used as a cyclical process to ensure continuous improvement of the organization.

4.6 Appreciative Inquiry for Highly Ready Organizations

Appreciative Inquiry (AI) is recommended for organizations that are stable and wish to empower employees for participation. AI focuses exclusively on the positive aspects of an organization and the relationships within the organization. The main idea of AI is to appreciate the positive core or strengths of the organization rather than to identify issues and their potential causes. AI adopts a well-known process called a 4D which is explained as follows:

■ *Discover*: OD practitioners enable members of the client organization to share stories and discover their "positive cores" (their values, beliefs, and strengths). The identification of the positive core starts with a pair of individuals, moves to groups, and is summarized at the organizational level.
■ *Dream*: After identifying the positive core, the OD practitioner inspires and enables everyone in the organization to brainstorm a positive future status for the organization, while making sure these ideas align across the organization.

- *Design*: OD practitioners enable organizational subgroups to develop a plan that will lead them to the future status they envisioned while brainstorming. Each member in the group develops a concrete plan at his or her level.
- *Destiny*: OD practitioners facilitate a conversation on how to implement the plan. After that, all organizational members carry out the plan. Periodically, members go through the cycle again and revise the outcomes of each phase.

Each phase of AI involves levels of assessment and feedback. In the discover phase, OD practitioners and members of the organization gather information about the positive core and share the results. In the dream phase, assessment is about the client's desired future, which is summarized and fed back to the whole group. In the design phase, plans at the group or organizational level are summarized and fed back to the group. In the destiny phase, ideas for effective implementation are gathered and shared with the group. So you can clearly see that assessment and feedback occurs throughout the AI process.

4.6.1 Vignette of Assessment Using Appreciative Inquiry

4.6.1.1 Situation

Family-run ABC (a pharmaceutical distribution company with 70 years of history), appointed a new CEO, Jerry. He is 40 years old and is the son of the previous CEO. ABC has approximately 100 employees in different functions such as transportation, sorting, sales, and support. The company has a low turnover rate, except for positions related to transportation and sorting. Throughout the last 70 years, the company has never had to lay anyone off, causing it to have a family-like culture.

ABC has constantly been ranked in the top five of their market, but has never been first. Jerry feels threats due to the changing laws and regulations of the industry, as well as saturation of the market resulting in lower margins and fierce competition. He calls in an OD consultant to diagnose the organization.

The OD consultant meets with all executives, team leaders, and a selected number of employees for a preliminary assessment. He quickly finds that the company is not well-structured, although its business has been very stable. ABC neither has mission and vision statements nor clear HR policies and procedures. One representative example is that they promote all employees sometimes. The OD consultant shares what he found with the CEO and requests the creation of an implementation team of six individuals involving key executives, middle managers, and front-line opinion leaders.

4.6.1.2 Processes of Assessing the Positive Core of the Organization

In the discover phase, the OD consultant gives the implementation team an assignment to complete an organizational environmental scan using the Political, Economic, Social, and Technological (PEST) Analysis. Once completed, the implementation team, including the CEO, goes on a two-day retreat with the OD consultant.

In the first session during the retreat, the group reviews the environmental analysis results and their implications for ABC. The goal of this session is to promote a sense of awareness regarding the current business environment and the need for change. Without pointing out any challenges of the organization, the consultant facilitates the creation of new mission, shared values, and core competencies' statements by asking the following questions:

■ Who are the customers of ABC?
■ What values does ABC provide to the customers?
■ What are the main activities of ABC?
■ What strengths do you have as an organization compared to the competitors?
■ What competitive values does ABC provide to its customers compared to the competitors?
■ What values have been most important at ABC?
■ What values should be kept and nurtured further?
■ What competencies must ABC develop further to be the No. 1 company in the industry?

After generating answers to the questions, participants are asked to prioritize answers and give explanations to each of the keywords defined for mission, shared values, and core competencies' statements.

After the two-day retreat, the results are shared with all employees in a survey format inviting further inputs from everyone in the organization. Results are then confirmed and finalized by having group meetings dividing all employees into four groups.

4.6.1.3 Outcomes

By incorporating the answers regarding its customers, values for customers, and main activities, a new mission statement for ABC is developed: "We provide total health care products and information to customers who are health care professionals and facilitate the creation of values for customers and employees through lifelong learning."

Core values for ABC based on the organization's history and the priority of organizational members are also developed as follows:

- Altruism—Help others; it will benefit us.
- Responsibility/ownership—Think and act as if they were my business.
- Professionalism—Complete tasks without giving up.
- Customer first—Treating customers is our top priority.
- Speed—Decide fast, act quickly.
- Challenge—Overcome any obstacles with confidence.
- Lifelong learning—Learn continually to generate added value.

Four core competencies of ABC are identified as follows:

- Lifelong learning
- Sales/marketing initiatives
- System initiatives
- Customer relationship management

4.6.1.4 Reflection

In this example, the discover phase as described above was implemented excellently. However, the OD consultant encountered a barrier of not believing in the power of dreaming beyond financial success. When facilitating the desired image of the company, the CEO insisted on focusing on financial growth, resulting in the lack of commitment from employees. The vision statement of "Run for 10 10 1 1," which means by 2010, among the top 10 companies in the field, we will become No. 1 for the increased rate of sales revenue and No. 1 in the increased rate of net profit, was created.

In the end, the OD effort at ABC made a positive impact on the organization in boosting pride among the employees. They felt a sense of direction by having a mutually agreed mission statement, and the core competency statements allowed top management to consciously focus on the innovation of core competencies. The core values' statement also served as a guide for sharing the culture of ABC.

When the company's progress was tracked two years after the OD effort, the number of employees was increased because of lowered turnover and the company grew its employee's development opportunities. Because of the power of participation of all employees in determining the positive core of the company, ABC applied the same AI process for its sister company.

4.7 Chapter Summary

Understanding environmental forces for change allows an organization to quickly develop ideas that can make a change effort successful. For that, using the force field analysis is encouraged. With concrete steps and the example in this chapter, you should now be able to conduct a force field analysis in your setting.

Assessing the level of readiness of the organization is another effective approach to OD. Sometimes change efforts fail because an organization is not ready for change. This chapter explored different stages of an organization in terms of its readiness. In addition, through the Great Place to Work Model, you were exposed to an ideal status of a highly participatory organization. Eight concrete steps to turning an organization from Level 1 (reactive) to Level 4 (high performing) are suggested. We also provided a real world example showing how one can assess an organization for its positive core using AI. We want to close with the reminder that when an organization performs at a satisfactory level, and there is a strong buy-in from the top, it is worthwhile to apply the AI approach for organizational assessment.

4.8 Tool for Practitioners: Force Field Analysis

Directions. Follow the steps and template below. By doing so, you will be able to develop strategies for a successful change initiative by reducing restraining forces, and keeping or increasing the level of driving forces.

Step 1. Define a change goal that will be served as a target for the analysis in the cell in the middle.

Step 2. Brainstorm and list the driving forces for the change goal on the left-hand side in the item section. Then, do the same thing for the restraining forces on the right-hand side.

Step 3. Record ratings of the potential impact of each item on the change initiative, using a 10-point Likert scale.

Driving Forces			A Change Goal	Restraining Forces		
Impact	Item	➡	Description	⬅	Impact	Item
		➡		⬅		
		➡		⬅		

Step 4. Reflect on the items for driving and restraining forces and their ratings. Create total scores for both forces and evaluate the current situation considering both forces.

	Driving Forces	*Restraining Forces*
Sum of Ratings		
Reflection		
Overall Evaluation		

Step 5. Brainstorm ideas to minimize restraining forces and to increase driving forces.

Ideas to Minimize Restraining Forces	*Ideas to Increase Driving Forces*
• •	• •

Step 6. By considering the potential impact of each of the brainstormed ideas for the success of the change initiative, develop concrete strategies (or goals) to manage the forces effectively.

■

■

Bibliography

Burchell, M., and Robin, J. 2011. *The Great Workplace: How to Build it, How to Keep it, and Why it Matters*. San Francisco: Jossey-Bass.

Farkas, M. G., and Hinchliffe, L. J. 2013. Library faculty and instructional assessment: Creating a culture of assessment through the high performance programming model of organizational transformation. *Collaborative Librarianship*, 5, 177–188.

Kish, L. 1982. Rensis Likert 1903–1981. *The American Statistician*, 36(2), 124–125.

Lewin, K. 1951. *Field theory in social science*. New York: Harper.

Likert, R. 1967. *The human organization*. New York: McGraw-Hill.

Miller, H. L. 1967. Participation of adults in education, a Force-Field Analysis. Retrieved from http://eric.ed.gov/?id=ED011996.

Nelson, L., and Burns, F. 1984. High-performance programming: A framework for transforming organizations. In J. Adams (Ed.), *Transforming work* (pp. 225–242). Alexandria, VA: Miles River Press.

Additional Online Resources

DePaul University/SNL Online. (n.d.). *Force Field Analysis*. Retrieved on January 15, 2016, from https://www.youtube.com/watch?v=64t_NIAG2QY.

Great Place to Work (n.d.). *Trust Index© Assessment*. Retrieved on January 18, 2016, from http://www.greatplacetowork.net/our-services/assess-your-organization/trust-index-assessment.

Great Place to Work U.S. (n.d.). *Want a great workplace? Learn how HR Valerie used the list application process to begin*. Retrieved on January 18, 2016, from https://www.youtube.com/watch?v=ouQG3OYIMGU (For more video resources on Great Place to Work, visit https://www.youtube.com/user/GreatPlacetoWorkUS).

Chapter 5

Planning for Assessment and Feedback for Organization Development

Jennifer L. Myers and Lindsay Weissberg

Contents

5.1 Introduction

In the previous chapter, organization development (OD) practitioners were introduced to models that address environmental forces and organizational readiness. This chapter introduces the importance of dedicating appropriate time and resources for planning assessment and feedback. We will discuss key concepts and literature to help you understand organizational assessment and feedback. Investing the appropriate time and resources during the planning stages of assessment and feedback is imperative; if not done properly, it cannot only negatively affect the data collection, but also the presentation of results during the feedback sessions. We will introduce key steps in planning for the assessment and what to consider when following these steps.

In this chapter, we will also identify the critical factors that demonstrate leadership buy-in. We will look critically at how the results should be presented to key stakeholders once in hand and offer suggestions on formal reporting. Finally, this chapter will introduce two short vignettes and provide a practical tool to help practitioners with planning for assessment and feedback.

5.2 The Importance of Planning for Assessment and Feedback

It is not only important for everyone involved in the planning, execution, and analysis of assessment to understand the benefits of planning for assessment and feedback, but also any individual who has a vested interest in the outcome. This includes employees, customers, and any other stakeholders.

Assessment is a critical tool for improving the processes of an organization and bringing to light the issues that exist, so leadership can take important steps in addressing them. The information gathered from assessments can drill down to issues not easily seen at the surface. In doing so, this can help leadership improve the capability and effectiveness of their day-to-day business operations. Therefore, the time and effort put into planning will affect the quality of the execution of the assessment and the participation. Why is this, you ask? You will need leadership buy-in if they did not initiate the assessment being conducted directly or if it is an initiative coming from corporate.

5.3 Planning for the Assessment

We have outlined the following nine steps that practitioners can use when planning for an OD assessment:

Step 1: Determine the goals of the assessment
Step 2: Consider your goals

Step 3: Determine the time of the assessment
Step 4: Location of the assessment
Step 5: Develop survey mapping
Step 6: Consult with stakeholders
Step 7: Incentive options
Step 8: Market Assessment—Get the word out
Step 9: Launch the assessment

Now that we have a quick reference list, let us look at these steps in more depth.

1. Determine the goals of the assessment:
   - What information are you seeking to elicit from your employees? If possible, connect this to organization's strategic initiatives and plans.
2. Considering your goals:
   - Determine the questions you will ask, and the format you will utilize. (Details related to diagnostic models can be found in Chapters 3 and 4, details on data collection methods are to follow in Chapter 6.)
3. Determine the time of the assessment:
   - Consider the time that will be allocated for employees to take the assessment. Remember factors such as high periods of vacation time usage, end of fiscal year, and high periods of customer demand.
4. Location of the assessment:
   - Determine where the assessment will be housed and delivered. If administered strictly through a web-based format, consider utilizing online survey vendors to ensure anonymity.
5. Develop survey mapping:
   - Based on the size of your organization, you may wish to review data by workgroup or by supervisor. Survey mapping allows for drill-down to the workgroup level. When using survey mapping, employees will receive a survey code to input when taking the assessment. The code will allow their results to be categorized according to workgroup, allowing for drill-down by supervisor, division, and so on. This allows for senior leaders to see what areas of the organization require greater levels of intervention.
6. Consult with stakeholders:
   - Stakeholders are those folks who may be your customers, labor partners, and key managers/supervisors. For your assessment goals, questions, and timing, remember having buy-in with the

organization's informal leaders will increase participation. When knowing and believing that their opinions are valued in survey development, they will be more likely to encourage their subordinates and peers that the assessment is valuable. Second, they will likely have valuable insight regarding survey administration that leaders have not considered.

7. Incentive options:
   - Consider the incentives you will offer employees to encourage participation in the assessment. While participation should be strictly voluntary, never coerced or required, many organizations offer their employees incentives. Table 5.1 discusses some valuable incentive options.

8. Market Assessment:
   - Advertise the upcoming assessment to the workforce. When in doubt, over-communicate utilizing verbal and written modalities. Items to consider in advertisements are the questions asked in the assessment, what leadership intends to do with the results (i.e., incorporate into upcoming strategic planning), incentives (see step 7), the dates of the survey, how the survey can be accessed, and who to contact with questions and concerns.

9. Launch the Assessment:
   - You have planned and now it is time to launch the assessment. Go for it!

5.4 Leadership Buy-in and Engaging the Workforce

Let us look at some of the critical factors that demonstrate strong leadership buy-in and support for assessments:

- *Factor 1*: Involvement in survey development, such as the questions asked and their format.
- *Factor 2*: Taking opportunities—both in person and in written communications—to discuss the importance of the assessment and plans for incorporating it into the organization's plans.
- *Factor 3*: Demonstrating what has been done with employee feedback in prior assessments or other forums for feedback.

Table 5.1   Incentive Options

Option	Useful for	To Whom	How	Examples
Small incentives	Participation Reminders	Everyone you wish to engage	No tracking needed, give to all participants	• Pens with survey link • Stress balls with links or administration dates • Small company logo items (USB drives, flash lights, etc.)
Large incentives	Participation Rewards	Workgroups with high participation	Utilizing workgroup mapping (see Step 5), you will know percentages of participation without identifiers to specific employee participation. To ensure anonymity, all employees in the workgroup—regardless of their individual participation in the survey—must receive the incentive.	• Tangible items, such as a catered lunch, vacation time, or large company logo items • Intangible items such as preferred parking, recognition in a corporate communication or at an employee event

▪ *Factor 4*: Encouraging leadership to communicate directly to the employees about the purpose and the importance of the assessment.
▪ *Factor 5*: Providing adequate resources to purchase the assessment tools and other related materials.

- *Factor 6*: Providing adequate resources and support for incentives to the workforce to encourage assessment participation.
- *Factor 7*: Ensuring that employees have protected time to take the assessment confidentially.

These factors demonstrate strong leadership buy-in and support for the assessment at hand because it means leadership is fully vested in the process and in the aftermath. Leadership should be involved before, during, and after the assessment. This not only demonstrates a genuine interest in what their employees' perspectives are, but also in leading the way for improvement. Leadership should be approachable and set aside protected time where their employees can talk to them in person and answer questions they may have. It is one thing to conduct the assessment and obtain buy-in from the employees, but the real test is what leadership does with the information gleaned from the assessment and how they communicate it back to their workforce. If this is not done or not done well, this will diminish the likelihood that future assessments will succeed. Building and sustaining that trust should be a critical element in all of this. If it is not, it will make your task as an OD practitioner more challenging and discourage trust among employees with their leadership.

Now, let us look a little closer at the fifth factor, providing adequate resources to purchase the assessment tools and other related materials. We must not only remember ourselves, but also ensure that leadership understands the absolute need for adequate resources and support when encouraging staff to participate in assessments. Employees are already strapped for time. Often they are overworked and sometimes even burned out. However, without question if this assessment is a priority for leadership, then they will provide protected time for their employees to complete the assessment, whether it takes five minutes or an hour. Executive leadership should ensure that all of their mid-level managers and frontline managers fall in line with this and are providing their employees this protected time. As we know, sometimes at the departmental level, not all initiatives are supported or provided follow-through by frontline supervisors in the way executive leadership intended, so follow-up and clear communication of expectations are needed prior to the formal launch of the assessment.

Let us also look at the important reasons why it is crucial to not only engage the workforce during the actual assessment but also during pre- and post-assessment period. Based on our collective experiences and working closely with leaders at various levels, we have pulled together Table 5.2 to elaborate on this point.

Table 5.2 Reasons to Engage Workforce during Assessment

Pre-Assessment	Assessment	Post-Assessment
Buy-in: This must be obtained first before anything should move forward. If employees and managers do not understand why they have been asked to take the survey, they simply will not participate and the critical information that would have followed will be lost.	Support: Encourage—but do not coerce—employees to participate in the assessment.	Consultant/Manager Meeting: Communicate the results of the assessment to leadership. What did leadership learn from their feedback?
Planning: If employees know about an assessment ahead of time, they will make sure they take the time out of their schedules to participate.	Availably: Be available for questions. Naturally, employees may have questions, so ensure you and your team are ready to answer them when called upon. This may be the difference between finishing the assessment and not.	Leadership/Employees: Leadership should be honest, sincere, and upfront about the results. This should take place soon after the assessment is completed and analyzed. Leadership should communicate directly to employees about the results of the assessment.
Marketing: This is a critical factor because employees must know that an assessment is available and the time the assessment will be open for them to complete it.	Purpose: Communicate *why* you want them to participate.	Recognition: Acknowledge the employees and frontline supervisors. Thank them for the time they took to take the assessment and welcome those who did not take it to consider doing so next time.

(*Continued*)

Table 5.2 (*Continued*)   Reasons to Engage Workforce during Assessment

Pre-Assessment	Assessment	Post-Assessment
Technology: If you are utilizing technology of any kind, troubleshoot and do a complete dry-run before launching the assessment to ensure you identify any problems before pushing it out facility wide. This will reduce or minimize major issues otherwise encountered by users.	Process: Communicate *how* to take the assessment. Utilize all avenues of communication— including e-mail, online, and in person. Clear instructions and uncomplicated/ nonlengthy assessments will be keys to whether or not the employee finishes the assessment. They may start it, but if it is not user-friendly, likelihood they will complete and submit it decreases.	Long-term action planning: Communicate leadership's action plan to address the concerns/ ideas brought forth in the assessment.

5.5 Identifying a Diagnostic Model and Data Collection Methods That Works Well for Your Organization

Each organization is different and approaches vary based on the structure, and that is why selecting the best model for the needs of your organization is critical. The diagnostic model you select for your organization will be an important decision, and as an OD practitioner, you will have to communicate why the chosen model is the best for your organization. Typically, leadership which has a vested interest in the results and a sincere reason for initiating the assessment will be interested, although there are exceptions, so it is better to be prepared when you have the very important meeting with them. When deciding upon models, Harrison and Shirom (1999) suggest that practitioners and consultants seek to meet at least two types of requirements. The first requirement applies to virtually all models in the applied behavior sciences. The second is more distinctive to those used in consulting organizational change specifically.

In Chapter 6, you will be introduced to several types of collection methods; for our purposes right now, we want to share with you why the selection of your data collection method is one of the most important decisions you will make during this entire process.

Data collection methods can often be overlooked in planning because most folks do not know the wide variety of methods that can be used or understand why selecting one over another can be the one decision that determines whether you collect valuable and applicable information to help improve processes within your organization. This lack of experience and knowledge can have dramatic impact on not only the outcome, but also on any future improvement opportunities identified through the assessment initiative. Careful selection of your data collection method(s) and instruments will reduce the likelihood for errors and accuracy.

5.6 Planning for Feedback—Presenting the Results

We have talked about the post-assessment in earlier pages of this chapter; now let us drill down further to the key players and things to consider when presenting the feedback and results. Again, we will get much deeper into this process in Chapter 7, but we would remiss if we did not spend time talking about the planning needed here as well.

In our experience, it is essential to ensure you have planned appropriately, and considered how to communicate to these groups of individuals about the results, and what it means to them specifically. We outline some tips for doing this in Table 5.3.

Rogers and Fong (2000) urge practitioners to consider both verbal presentations and verbal–visual presentation. "Brief short presentations to an executive officer ought to include a bullet page or an outline that states the facts and findings" (p. 49). Depending on your audience, determine what type and how long the presentation will be. You do not want to lose your audience before you present the results, therefore, the planning for feedback stage should be well thought-out and methodical in execution. I like what Peter Block has said in the past about sorting through information collected, "The picture you present should focus on a few central aspects of the problem or possibility. The mistake with most presentations is that they are too long and too intricate" (p. 230).

Whether or not you are an outside OD consultant or internal practitioner, you have been hired to sort through the information and present it in a clear and understandable manner. You may have leadership who wants a report written with the findings of the assessment, so it is important to be prepared for this. This may be something of an Executive Summary Report or a report that is much more extensive.

Table 5.3 Planning for Communication at Different Levels

Who	What
Presenting Results— Executive Leadership	During the early planning stages, it is critical to ensure leadership is on board and there is a clear readiness for assessment and feedback. This should be apparent before launching. Once feedback is received from your workforce, it is then time to appropriately organize, analyze, and communicate the results to leadership and key players.
Presenting Results— Managers	Frontline managers and supervisors have a very important role because they will be the link between leadership communication of the assessment results and after action planning that must take place. Therefore, they should feel informed and ask questions as needed.
Presenting Results— Employees	The results of the assessment must be shared with employees at all levels of the organization. Leadership must determine how this should be accomplished. Leadership must also determine the programs and/or policies they will implement because of the feedback. Action plans and other similar approaches can map implementation.

You will need to ask the executive leadership specifically what they want before the assessment begins.

Your Executive Summary Report should include at least these categories and others depending on the organization-specific requests. Again, we will get much deeper into this topic in Chapter 7, but as you plan, you need to ensure you are thinking about this final step and asking the right questions to ensure you know what data must be collected to give your client or your organization the findings they need to build a proper action plan:

1. Title
2. Overview
3. Goals of assessment
4. Process and methods
5. Results of assessment (findings)
6. Conclusions and guidance to a solution (OD-related)

The above categories may be further broken down and reported on by executive leadership. You should know what leadership wants from you in the way of reporting results to them and their expectations on post-assessment involvement in presenting results to their workforce.

5.7 Vignette 1: Addressing Assessment Participation Challenges

It is likely that most, if not all organizations, especially those that are very large in size will want a large percentage of their employees to participate in surveys being conducted annually. However, many companies face the dreaded lack of participation by their workforce. This could be for several reasons, but regardless of what they are, it is up to senior leaders to employ strategies to not only engage their workforce and motivate them to participate, but also to provide employees psychological safety so they feel comfortable in participating. This vignette will closely examine strategies practitioners and senior leaders have put in place to resolve these issues.

A sizeable organization comprising several thousand employees encountered challenges when conducting a large-scale assessment where feedback was both wanted and needed from employees. Year after year, the same problems persisted: misperceptions of what the assessment was for, mistrust of leadership's intentions with the data, lack of time to complete the assessment, lack of interest and understanding of what the purpose of the assessment was, and others. With the past in mind, leadership pulled in a team of OD professionals to examine the presenting issues and propose solutions to counteract prior year challenges.

Some of the major solutions implemented and improved upon were as follows:

1. Better communication among leadership and employees
2. Demonstration of support for the assessment by leadership
3. Increased visibility by leadership
4. Improved marketing strategies that were informative but also light-hearted and humorous
5. Expansion of assessment tools and ways to take the assessment
6. Recruitment of motivated frontline staff within each department line to be additional points of contacts and information bearers concerning the assessment

The result increased participation by nearly 10%, which equals several hundred employees and exceeded leadership's goals.

5.8 Vignette 2: Following up on Assessment Results

It is tempting for leaders to review assessment results, perhaps have moments of reflection, and then move on to the next item on their to-do list. Employee assessments are meaningless if senior leadership does not take the results seriously and act upon them in a way that is visible to all employees. This vignette will discuss why following up on assessment results is essential, and ways to demonstrate follow-up to your staff.

A nationwide organization implemented an annual employee assessment approximately 10 years ago. The assessment received much publicity from top leaders, who heavily encouraged employee participation. While in earlier years of conducting the survey, administration garnered high participation rates; they gradually waned over the years. While this can be attributed to a myriad of factors, including survey fatigue and low employee morale, employees in part attributed the decreased participation to the lack of results. After years of dutifully taking the assessment, they perceived no change in the organization. This was also reflected in the scores, as they had gradually decreased. Meanwhile, senior leaders took the results seriously. They poured hours of time into analyzing the results and drilling them down to specific areas in the workforce. They developed action plans to address the lowest scoring questions, and even asked department heads to develop their own action plans based on their drilled-down survey results. Despite these efforts, employees saw no visible results. What happened?

Several factors contributed to this general employee perception. First, neither a comprehensive analysis of the assessment results nor action plans were communicated to frontline employees. While they received the raw survey data, employees received little guidance on how to interpret the results or how the data had trended. Action plans were not widely distributed to employees. While posted to an employee webpage, the organizational action plans were not aggressively communicated to employees. Second, action plans did not receive long-lasting support from organizational leadership. While leaders supported their development, they did not follow-up on their implementation throughout the year, giving rise to the famous quote "the best laid plans of mice and men often go awry"—meaning detailed plans are futile when the ability or desire to execute them is unclear.

Leaders at this organization made a critical error with lasting impact on assessment participation and employee morale: they did not show frontline employees that the assessment results mattered to them. This was primarily achieved through failure to communicate and translate the results, and through failure to connect survey results to changes made in the organization. This led to reduced survey participation and lower survey scores in future years.

Organizational leaders can choose from many avenues when determining how to avoid these common pitfalls. Leaders must recognize that they will likely not have the time to own the entire assessment process, and should delegate administration responsibilities to a reliable, high-performing staff member or team. Leaders must set a clear vision, and indicate that employee assessment is a year-round responsibility. The assigned staff member or team will then oversee all employee communication efforts, action-plan tracking, and enforcement. Leaders must remember to tie the survey results to the organization's vision and strategic plan, and when there are linkages, to visibly draw them. Employees will not assume their voices are heard unless their leadership provides that direct indication and inference.

5.9 Chapter Summary

The effort you take to plan will be an investment well worth the time. The planning you are doing for the assessment will help you to identify potential challenges and unforeseen problems you otherwise may not have realized were waiting for you. It is an opportunity to recognize them early and resolve them before launching the assessment. Often you, the OD practitioner, are the key to a successful assessment and the greatest tool leadership has in not only executing the assessment well but also in communicating the results post-assessment. You have the knowledge and the experience that will help the organization to collect useful information that will be the building blocks to solutions and future action-planning.

5.10 Tool for Practitioners

Overview Checklist *Planning is important when organizations are preparing for an assessment of any kind, especially those that are large in scale. Planning is a critical step for OD practitioners to guide their organizations through this process smoothly*	
The scale of this assessment will be as follows:	
	Entire organization
	Selected departments within the organization
	Selected divisions within the departments of the organizations
	A single program or workgroup
	Individual job-level
	Other
The primary focus of this assessment is as follows:	
	Talent management
	New employee on-boarding and orientation
	Perceptions of organizational leadership
	Process improvement and systems redesign
	Employee engagement
	Strategic planning
	Customer satisfaction
	Other
These assessment model(s) will be used as follows:	
	Marvin Weisbord Six-Box model
	Open systems model
	Closed systems model
	Causal model of organizational performance and change
	The 7-S model
	Other

These assessment methods will be used as follows:	
	Brief survey (10 questions or less)
	Extensive survey (10 questions or more)
	Focus groups
	Interviews
	SWOT (strength, weaknesses, opportunities, and threats)
	Self-assessments
	Other
The timeframe for this assessment is anticipated to be as follows:	
	Less than five days
	5 days to 15 days
	15 days to 30 days
	30 days to 60 days
	60 days to 90 days
	Other
This assessment has the support of executive leadership as follows:	
	Yes
	No
This assessment has the support of departmental leadership as follows:	
	Yes
	No

Bibliography

Block, P. 2011. *Flawless Consulting: A Guide to Getting Your Expertise Used.* San Francisco, CA: Jossey-Bass.

Harrison, M., and Shirom, A. 1999. *Organizational Diagnosis and Assessment: Bridging Theory and Practice.* Thousand Oaks, CA: Sage.

Rogers, R., and Fong, J. 2000. *Organizational Assessment: Diagnosis and Intervention.* Amherst, MA: HRD Press.

Chapter 6

Collecting and Analyzing Data for Organization Development

Angela L.M. Stopper and Jennifer L. Myers

Contents

6.1 Introduction

Now that we have discussed the basic concepts related to organization development (OD) diagnosis and assessment, the models that can successfully undertake it, and the steps needed to properly plan for a successful engagement, this chapter will focus specifically on the tools and techniques needed for collecting and analyzing data to turn that data from a building block into information with context and meaning that can be used in a successful OD engagement.

First, let us set the stage by cautioning you; collecting and analyzing data are not always as straight forward as we would like to think. This is because practitioners, and leadership, need to understand the data needs and the organizational structure to determine what methods will work best for their unique organization. They also need to consider the OD engagement they are trying to undertake and what data they will need to undertake it. This is often a different question than "what data can be easily collected?" Do you see the difference? Just because something is easy to collect, does not make it relevant for every organization in every OD situation. However, even though data collection is not always easy, it need not be difficult. Part of what can make it easier is planning for assessment, which was discussed in great depth in the previous chapter.

So now, let us look below at the differences between collecting any data and collecting relevant, decision-quality data.

6.2 Any Data versus Relevant Data

In this, "the age of information," we all know that you can collect a plethora of data about any single topic. What becomes important is ensuring the data you collect will be useful to your particular situation. This is why we encourage you to think about the importance of individualized data collection and analysis. We contend this step is necessary to make the data gathered in this stage of an OD engagement meaningful to your team.

As practitioners, we can easily fall victim to data overload while moving through an OD assessment exercise. This happens for several reasons, some of which stem from poor planning and lack of understanding of the end goal. But there are also well-intentioned causes of data overload. Overambitious and overachieving staff can collect an abundance of data when tasked to, all simply to show their managers or others at the top that they are doing a good job. So the first step in collecting and analyzing data must revolve around defining what needs to be collected and why.

Whether you are a practitioner, consultant, researcher, or manager, you should ensure there is sound reason for collecting the data requested and a sound strategy for what you will do with the data once it is collected. Not only what you will do with the data once you have collected it, but what variables the data will answer in your overall OD plan. By being purposeful in defining why different data points are impactful in the overall OD exercise, you ensure you are collecting relevant, decision-quality data you can then put context and meaning to, in order to create information. It is one thing to know how to collect data, it is another to understand how to analyze it, and help leadership to understand the results so they can implement positive change based upon what you discover.

6.3 The Importance of Planning for Data Integration

Numerous methods are acceptable for collecting data in an OD engagement. Some of the most commonly used methods include:

- Interviews
- Focus groups
- Surveys or questionnaires
- Observations
- Examinations of records

Later in this chapter, we will discuss some examples of each of the above methods, and you can find additional resources at the end of this chapter to help you in finding and using each.

6.4 Collecting Organization Data

During the planning process, you should have already taken time to think about the anticipated outcomes of your engagement. In thinking about those anticipated outcomes, it now becomes important to define what kind of data you will need, and considering the structure of the organization, what methods of data collection will give you that data.

In organizations where individuals are not used to speaking out in large groups, focus groups might not be the best data collection tool. Adversely, in an organization that is extremely geographically diverse, face-to-face interviews might be cost prohibitive. Start by considering each data gathering method and rating them on an organization-specific scale on six key variables: efficiency, objectivity, comparability, completeness, accuracy, and flexibility. If the method chosen does not score "At least 75% of the time" in all factors, you may wish to reconsider your data collection method or pair it with a second or third method in order to reach close to scores of "Nearly all of the time" for each factor.

6.4.1 Efficiency

In this context, efficiency relates to your ability, as the data collection agent, to efficiently engage with the stakeholders using the selected method. Will the method enable or encumber you as you engage with stakeholders?

6.4.2 Objectivity

In this context, objectivity relates to your ability, as the data collection agent, to use the selected method to gather data in the most objective way possible, eliminating as much potential for bias as possible. To measure this variable, ask yourself "will the method I have chosen ensure that I collect data without my preconceived opinions making an impact?"

6.4.3 Comparability

In this context, comparability relates to your ability, as the data collection agent, to gather data that can be compared, and if that comparison will lead you to reasonable assumptions. The old saying "you cannot compare apples to oranges" holds true, even in the OD context. To evaluate this variable, ask yourself "will the method I have chosen give me enough data points so that I can see the current state and make decisions that lead to a desired state?"

6.4.4 Completeness

In this context, completeness relates to your ability, as the data collection agent, to use the chosen method to gather all of the data you need to make an evaluation of the current state and design a road map for moving to the desired state. Will the method provide you with enough data, will the data provided be complete and compelling? (As a side note here, you will often have to choose more than one data collection method to ensure you achieve 100% on this variable.)

6.4.5 Accuracy

In this context, accuracy relates to your ability, as the data collection agent, to use the chosen method to collect correct, true, factual data, not simply assumptions and opinions. Will the method you have chosen allow you to get a honest picture of the current state of events? If collecting data from individuals, trust will be an essential piece of the accuracy puzzle (has trust been established in you, as the data collection agent, to allow individuals to paint a true picture of events for you?). If collecting data from systems, are the outputs trustworthy representations of the data (are computer programs current and virus free? are tools properly collaborated? etc.).

6.4.6 Flexibility

In this context, flexibility relates to your ability, as the data collection agent, to have the time and range needed to collect all data that relates to the engagement. Again, will the method enable or encumber you as you engage with stakeholders in each area deemed relevant to the data collection needs.

In the end, you will come up with a method appraisal much like what is shown in Figure 6.1. In fact, you can use Figure 6.1 as a template to design your own worksheet.

Data Collection Method		Not at al	25% of the time	50% of the time	75% of the time	Nearly all of the time
Formal Interviews						
Variable	**Need**					
Efficiency	I need to quickly question all 15 line supervisors.		x			
Scheduling of interview with 15 individuals will be time consuming. I know I can speak to individuals here in headquarters quickly, but other may be harder.						
Less than 75%? How will you increase? • I will use a scheduling service such as doodle in order to quickly schedule these meetings. • I will ask my supervisor for one additional support person in the beginning of this project who will be tasked directly with scheduling of interviews.						
Objectivity	I need to ensure my bias doesn't change the opinions offered by the supervisors.					x
Using a formal interview protocol, I will be able to ensure a reasonable removal of bias.						
Less than 75%? How will you increase? n/a						
Comparability	I need to be able to gather data from each supervisor to see where similarities exist.					x
By using a formal method, speaking individually to each supervisor, and recording and transcribing the interviews, I will be able to gather their thoughts to compare on my own after the fact.						
Less than 75%? How will you increase? n/a						
Completeness	I need to be able to gather data that will allow me to determine next steps.					x
Using a formal interview process, I will be able to gather data to questions I generate in advance in order to get me the information I need.						
Less than 75%? How will you increase? n/a						
Accuracy	I need to collect correct, true, factual data.			x		
I know and trust that supervisors will be honest with me in answering my questions. There may be some who hold back because of fear of ramifications because of the face-to-face proximity.						
Less than 75%? How will you increase? • I can support this data gathering method with a method that isn't face-to-face. I will compare results to ensure I have collected accurate information.						

Figure 6.1 Picking the right data-gathering method worksheet. *(Continued)*

Flexibility	I need to speak to supervisors at both headquarters as well as regional offices.					x
Using Skype, I can ensure my face-to-face interviews are completed consistently at all offices, regardless of location.						
Less than 75%? How will you increase? n/a						

Final Evaluation
A formal interview process will work well in this data collection, but to increase efficiency and accuracy, I will: • Use scheduling technology   • Request the help of a scheduling assistant   • Use an anonymous internet based survey to the same population to check reliability

Figure 6.1 (Continued)   Picking the right data-gathering method worksheet.

6.5 Data Collection Methods

To help you decide which methods will work best in your own data collection, we want to now define each method and discuss the positives and challenges for each.

But before we get into that, let's take a minute to talk about questions. Do you know how to write a good interview/survey/focus group question? Did you read the previous question and realize it was a poorly written question?

6.5.1 Open versus Closed Questions

We joke in the previous section, asking a question and then calling the question out as a poorly constructed question. Now, we will tell you why.

When writing questions for data collection, there are two basic concepts you need to understand. To put the differences simply, a closed question can be answered with one word. An open question engages the interviewee (or focus group or survey taker) to express their opinions in more than one word. In our previous example, the question was asked: Do you know how to write a good interview/survey/focus group question? In thinking about the differences between closed and open questions, you can see this is a closed question. The person being interviewed could answer this question with a quick "yes" or "no" and satisfy the questioner. Sometimes a simple yes or no is all we are looking for, and intentionally writing a closed question is fine. But more often, as OD practitioners, the "why" is important. So we need to consider using open questions instead.

Can the above question be turned into an open question? Sure! (See that, another closed question. Maybe a better way to ask it would have been, "How do we change a closed question to be an open question that gets us the deeper knowledge for which we're looking?").

Let's look at a few examples in Table 6.1.

We threw that last one in just to show you open questions do not always need to be longer. Short or long, the goal of a good open question is to pull out the data you need to make decisions (to gather decision-quality data). If your question must be followed by "Why," it is probably a closed question, and you should consider rewriting it (see Table 6.2 for an example).

Table 6.1   A Comparison of Open versus Closed Questions

Closed Question	Open Question
Do you know how to write a good interview question?	Describe the steps you take to ensure you are writing good interview questions.
Do you feel supported by management?	Describe for me a time when you felt that management fully supported your work and cared about your success. What specific steps had they taken to make you feel that way?
Can you describe your perfect work day?	Please describe your perfect work day.
Do you like coming to work?	What aspects of your job make you happy to come to work?
Do management's safety rules impact your day?	How do management's safety rules impact your day?

Table 6.2   A Closed Question That Deserves a Rewrite

Closed Question	Rewrite to an Open Question
Do you enjoy your work here? Why?	Think of a time when you really enjoyed working here. Describe for me what specifically happened that made you feel that way.

Writing good questions takes practice. We often write how we talk, and we talk using closed ended questions. Are you having a nice day? Nice weather, right? Did you see the game last night? All of these are often used as ice breakers to start a conversation. In an OD data-gathering situation, skip the small talk and get to the point. That does not mean you can ignore the rapport building step in interviews, focus groups, surveys, or the like. Instead, use the ice breaker to gather more data.

A good opening question is "Let's start by you telling me a bit about yourself/your typical day/your ideal management situation, etc." Let the individual open up to you in what is still an open question way and then dive in. However, if you insist on using a closed question in your interview protocol, this is the one and only time we would suggest that it might be appropriate. For an opening question, you could say "*Can you* tell me a little bit about yourself?" Since this is your first question, asking rather than telling someone what to do might be appropriate. Your ability to build rapport with the participant and trust with them starts with the level of respect you show out of the gate. Small changes can have tremendous impact, so judge what is needed for each situation. Just know that with a closed question, such as "*Can you* tell me a little bit about yourself?" you might receive a short answer of "no" and will need to have a recovery plan in place.

So, why don't we use open questions all of the time? Well, sometimes it is more difficult to say "tell me about a time when something good/bad happened." You feel like people will feel put on the spot. From years of experience, I can tell you that is hardly the case. And where people do not have specific examples, they will often say "you know, I don't remember a time when xyz, but let me tell you about abc" which is often just as useful.

Five Tips to writing open questions are as follows:

1. Do not be afraid to use open questions.
2. Ask what you want to know, small talk is not necessary.
3. Avoid starting questions with Can or Do. Instead use What or How.
4. Read your questions and see if they can be answered in one word. If so, consider rewriting them.
5. Consider doing a test interview/focus group/survey with a colleague before the actual data-gathering event to ensure your questions are getting you the data you desire.

Now that we have discussed question writing, let's dive into the different methods for data collection.

6.5.2 Interviews

There are several ways to conduct an interview. According to Gupta et al. (2007), "Interviews can be conducted in person, by phone, or by computer technology (such as online cameras, video conferencing, and instant messaging)" (p. 45). A benefit to conducting a phone interview is that even in remote locations, the interviewer and interviewee can still connect. However, it can also put you at a disadvantage because you lose the face-to-face contact that would normally occur. Gupta et al. (2007) explained other disadvantages to the phone interview, "Because most people will refuse to participate in long phone interviews, phone interviews are typically scheduled to last no longer than 30 minutes. Such time limitations clearly reduce the amount of information that can be gathered" (p. 45).

It is assumed by some that interviews are one of the easiest ways to collect data about learning and performance, but in reality, they can be one of the most challenging methods of data collection because of the level of skill and knowledge required by the interviewer (Gupta et al. 2007). Glesne (2006) points out, "The questions you bring to your interview are not set within a binding contract; they are your best effort before you have had the chance to use them with a number of respondents" (p. 79).

In data collection for OD, there are four types of interviews that can be used:

- Informal interviews: Conversation not using interview protocols or other formal tools.
- Formal interviews: Structured interviews, designed to formally collect data from a population.
- Open-ended interviews: A form of formal interview where open-ended questions are asked to the population to gather deep knowledge on why someone feels the way he/she does.
- Close-ended interviews: A form of formal interview where close-ended questions (yes or no; rate this statement on a provided scale) are asked to gather broad knowledge on agreement or dissension on selected points.

We will explore each in greater detail now.

Informal interviews are merely conversations. In an informal interview structure, the data collection agent simply moves through an organization and talks to people. A script is not used, nor is an interview protocol. See Table 6.3 for some of the positives and challenges of using this method.

Considering the list of positives and negatives (see Table 6.3), it is often suggested that informal interviews be used simply as an opening exercise in any OD initiative. While these kinds of discussions can give you some good data about where more digging must be done, they are rarely used in the true data-gathering process. Formal interviews are far more structured and better for that. Again, formal interviews can fall into one of two categories, open-ended or close-ended. Let's look at both.

In an open-ended interview, the data collection agent generates a topic outline about the problem or issue to be investigated based on input from the change sponsor. This outline is used to guide the interviews. When using an open-ended interview structure, have the change sponsor review and approve the draft topic outline. One should also have informants in the organization review and approve the draft, to ensure the interview outline is in keeping with the culture of the organization.

You can think of open-ended interviews as qualitative research. The qualitative research approach asks open-ended rather than yes-or-no questions to enable people to explain their thoughts, feelings, or beliefs. Data gathered in this manner can yield insights into worker perceptions and attitudes, but the findings can rarely be applied to the whole organization because the sample size is often too small. So, open-ended interview results are suggestive rather than definitive. The insights generated by them are often explored further through quantitative research, which provides reliable, hard statistics. See Table 6.4 for a summary of the pros and cons of using open-ended interviews for data gathering.

Table 6.3   Pros and Cons of Using Informal Interviews

Positives of Using Informal Interviews	Challenges of Using Informal Interviews
Little to no prep is needed	Data collected may be scattered and incomplete
Interviews are not as rigid	It is easy to lose track of time
Data that may not have come out in a more structured conversation does	Lack of structure causes misdirected conversations (side tracking; rabbit holing)

Table 6.4   Pros and Cons of Open-Ended Interviews

Positives of Using Open-Ended Interviews	Challenges of Using Open-Ended Interviews
Typically not leading	Can be more complicated to code and analyze due to the length of some answers
Unlimited possible answers	It is easy to lose track of time
More detail and clarity	Lack of structure causes misdirected conversations (side tracking; rabbit holing)
Encourages complete and meaningful responses	Lack of structure makes interviews hard to compare one-to-one because different data can come up every time

For close-ended interviews, the second type of formal interview, the data collection agent is first tasked with preparing a list of questions with scaled responses. This allows you, as the researcher, to pose the same questions in the same way to all respondents. This then allows results to be analyzed using statistics, which can give the strongest data, depending on the determined needs. Additional positives and challenges of using this data collection method are outlined in Table 6.5.

You can think of close-ended interviews as quantitative research. The qualitative research method uses close-ended questions, enabling the

Table 6.5   Pros and Cons of Close-Ended Interviews

Positives of Using Close-Ended Interviews	Challenges of Using Close-Ended Interviews
Easier for participants to answer	Participants who wish to elaborate typically cannot because responses are more simplistic
Ability to respond more quickly	Short answers provide limited details behind "why" someone answers as they do
Less likely to get responses not related to the question	Limited to no opportunity to explore the reasons behind a response
Fewer issues for participants when answering	When written improperly, questions can lead
Responses are easier to code and analyze	Responses may not represent a full range of answers that may come up in less-structured dialogues

researcher to determine the exact percentage of people who answer *yes* or *no* to a question or who selected answer *a*, *b*, *c*, or *d* using a Likert scale.

Interviews can gather data for many OD initiatives. Remember, interviews can also be conducted in many ways: in person, by phone, or by computer technology (such as online cameras, video conferencing, and instant messaging (Gupta et al. 2007). Do not limit yourself to one way of interviewing. If you are using interviews in an appreciative inquiry (AI) OD initiative, you can use open-ended questions such as these to build a picture of the organization:

- *(Can you)* Tell me a story about a time when you felt most motivated and encouraged in your job and in your organization.
- What was happening?
- When did this happen?
- By job title, who was involved?
- For what reason(s) do you feel you were so motivated and encouraged?

6.5.3 Focus Groups

Another very common qualitative research techniques for gathering data is the use of a focus group. Gupta et al. (2007) state that "In the focus group interview method, people who have something in common are brought together and asked their opinions and ideas about a specific topic. Most focus groups are made up of five to eight people" (p. 46).

A key element of conducting a focus group is having a highly skilled and prepared facilitator (Gupta et al. 2007). "Neutrality is important in order that the facilitator's focus remain on the process, not the outcome" (Kolb 2011, p. 4). Kolb's advice to facilitators is to not become concerned about the issue at hand or become vested in its outcome because too much involvement along these lines can distract, causing an unwanted impact on procedural choices made by the facilitator.

So again, in focus group research, a moderator leads a discussion among a small group of individuals who have been deemed as important information sources for the initiative. This research method can be used in various settings and can be very beneficial in collecting important data. The ability of the facilitator is critical and anyone acting in such a role should be very experienced when conducting focus groups.

Focus groups work best when kept short (about one hour or less) and focused on just a few questions (1–3). You can think of focus groups as group interviews. Just as in informal interviews, informal focus groups are simply group conversations focused around a problem. Formal focus groups, just like interviews, can be open-ended or close-ended and many of the same rules apply. Besides the positives and challenges that mirror those from the interview discussion, focus groups have some additional as shown in Table 6.6.

6.5.4 Surveys

Another very common quantitative research technique for gathering data is the use of surveys. Surveys allow a researcher to gather the opinions of many people in a very structured way. "Developing good surveys is difficult. Following a systematic process helps to ensure that the objectives and desired results are achieved" (Gupta et al. 2007, p. 51). John Creswell, a leading author and researcher in survey design suggested considering the following:

1. Identify the purpose of the research. The purposes generalize from a sample to a population so inferences can be made about some characteristic, attitude, or behavior of the population.
2. Indicate why a survey is the preferred data collection procedure for the study.

Table 6.6   Pros and Cons of Focus Groups

Positives of Using Focus Groups	Challenges of Using Focus Groups
Quickly gather data from multiple sources	Group think
Nonverbal responses can be observed and analyzed	Strong personalities can dominate and direct the conversation
Interaction can take place between facilitator/practitioner and participants	Participants may experience perceived peer pressure to agree with others in the group
Strong facilitators can move the conversation forward and make participants feel comfortable	Challenging to facilitate group discussion and stay on topic

3. Indicate whether the survey will be cross-sectional—with the data collected at one point in time—or whether it will be longitudinal—with data collected over time.
4. Specify the form of data collection (Creswell 2013, p. 157).

Surveys, just like interviews and focus groups, can be formal or informal using open-ended or close-ended questions. Because many of the same positives and challenges exist between informal surveys as do for informal interviews, let's focus on close-ended surveys for the remainder of this discussion. Table 6.7 shows the comparison.

Again, the Likert scale is the most commonly used way of scaling responses on a close-ended survey. In the Likert scaling method, respondents are asked to indicate their response to a statement using a scale that runs from positive to negative or negative to positive. Depending on how the response scale is written, respondents can either be forced to choose whether they feel more positively or negatively or be allowed to indicate a neutral position. Let's look at an example of each in Figure 6.2.

There are many arguments about which option is better and which is more effective (a forced choice scale or a neutral choice scale). An OD practitioner may prefer a forced choice scale, because it is more definitive. An employee may prefer a scale allowing him or her the ability to provide a neutral opinion, because sometimes it is easier to just be neutral instead of committing to one feeling or another.

Table 6.7   Pros and Cons of Close-Ended Surveys

Positives of Using Close-Ended Surveys	*Challenges of Using Close-Ended Surveys*
A large mass of people can be reached	Responses are limited
Data are more easily interpreted because you do not have long transcriptions of interview data	Follow-up and clarifying questions are not possible
Findings can be statistically validated	It can be a challenging task to create a good survey
There are numerous tools and technologies available now to assist researchers in creating surveys	Practitioners may want to use a forced choice response list, where participants may prefer a neutral choice being available

```
┌─────────────────────────────────────────────────────────────────────┐
│  I am enjoying learning about Likert scales                           │
│                                                                       │
│  Strongly disagree   Somewhat disagree   Disagree    Agree    Somewhat agree   Strongly agree │
│        ○                    ○                ○          ○            ○               ○         │
└─────────────────────────────────────────────────────────────────────┘
```

```
┌─────────────────────────────────────────────────────────────────────┐
│  I am enjoying learning about Likert scales                           │
│                                                                       │
│    Strongly disagree    Disagree    Neither disagree nor agree    Agree    Strongly agree │
│          ○                 ○                  ○                     ○            ○         │
└─────────────────────────────────────────────────────────────────────┘
```

Figure 6.2   Examples of a Likert survey question using a forced choice scale and a neutral choice scale.

Let's think about this conundrum with an example with which we are all familiar. Think about your high-school grading system. At the end of the year, the learner can earn an *A*, *B*, *C*, *D*, or an *F* in his or her classes. *C* is the middle, *C* is average, and *C* is comfortable. If we added *E* to the scale, suddenly, there would be no middle, no average, and everyone would either be on the high half of the scale or on the low half. That sorting can make people very uncomfortable.

Neither choice has been proven to be right. It is up to survey designers to decide which scale they want to use. The important thing is to know the difference and choose based on a logical reason.

Besides the old pen and paper survey, surveys can also be administered online using web-based services. There are advantages and disadvantages to using technology to gather survey data. One advantage is that with modern survey techniques, you can delve deeper into questions than you could with a pen and paper survey. Online surveys can be created that update the question set depending on the answers received. This gives the survey respondent a more customized survey depending on their answers, and allows for deeper data to be gathered.

Additionally, online survey tools often include data analysis software, so results are quickly collated and available for review. With the advancement of technology and online resources, collection methods can be less complicated; utilizing these advancements can benefit a researcher greatly.

Group decision technology has also enabled us to take the simple online survey to the next level. In a group decision exercise supported by technology, software is used to enable a group of individuals the ability to record responses to a question set in real time. The software shows the collation of the answers to the group. A facilitator can then lead the group through the learnings to come to a real-time decision. Group decision software is available for free on the internet or companies can be hired to lead organizations through such exercises.

In the end, each step should be considered carefully when utilizing the survey method and followed carefully. Preparation is a key to ensuring that the other steps are executed properly and smoothly. However, even with technology, an organization can face an uphill climb to gain participation depending on the challenges that exist within its own, unique culture.

6.5.4.1 Real-World Themed Vignette

Now, let's take a minute to explore a real-world themed vignette on this topic of increasing participation in employee surveys.

Astro Energy was started as a family-run oil exploration and drilling firm headquartered in Houston, Texas. Over the years, Astro expanded with offshore rigs throughout the Gulf of Mexico and recently started expansion into parts of Central and South America through partnerships and buy-outs. As a growing multinational organization, Astro realizes that employee engagement is a key to keeping their strong corporate culture alive.

As such, headquarters have created an employee engagement survey and released it to all workers with an e-mail sent straight from Mr. Longhorn (the CEO) himself. In receiving the results, human resources (HR) first reported a 70% response rate. Mr. Longhorn was pleased, but asks for more information. He would like to see how response rates on the off-short rigs compare to those in the new international locations and headquarters. All of a sudden, his team tells him there is not enough data to make a good comparison.

Mr. Longhorn is confused. How can 70% not be enough? Longing for answers, he calls for help. Mr. Longhorn remembers an article he read months earlier about increasing employee engagement. He looks up the article and calls the OD consultant who wrote the article.

Together, they built a plan:

Step 1: Fully understand the depth of the data collected
Step 2: Determine where data gaps are present

Step 3: Determine the significance of gaps
Step 4: Collect additional data
Step 5: Develop a plan to close significant gaps

Step 1: Fully understand the depth of the data collected.
Upon review of the raw data that were collected from the survey, it is discovered that while the response rate from headquarters employees was 98%, the combined response rate from the international offices was 12% of employees. From the rigs, it was even less hovering right at 8%.

Step 2: Determine where data gaps are present.
By seeing this data distribution by location, the team is able to discover that the initial high response rate came about because almost 100% of the headquarters employees completed the survey, while the smaller teams away from headquarters did not engage.

Step 3: Determine the significance of gaps.
The team and Mr. Longhorn discuss the data gap. Mr. Longhorn restates his interest in ensuring Astro continues to have a strong corporate culture. He feels this is critical, especially considering the corporate expansion strategy (partnerships and buy-outs). For these reasons, it is determined that the discovered data gap is significant and must be addressed.

Step 4: Collect additional data.
To address the gap, the team determines they must discover what is causing the low participation. They decide to use structured focus groups to collect information quickly, because time is of the essence. They pull together groups of senior leaders and front-line supervisors at the international offices and on the rigs and ask questions designed to get the managers to share their thoughts on why participation is so low.

Through these discussions, it is discovered that the following two major challenges exist that have impacted the percentage of employees who completed the survey:

1. To take the survey, employees had to log into a computer and navigate the instructions to gain access.
   a. Due to various employee occupations, not all employees log into or utilize computers frequently.
   b. Since the survey and instructions were written in English, some of the remote employees were not comfortable navigating the instruction or the survey itself, and certainly did not feel prepared to provide their input.

2. There was little knowledge of and interest in the survey outside of
   headquarters where Mr. Longhorn's larger-than-life personally was well
   known and well loved.
   a. Not all employees fully knew what the survey was or were available
      to take it during its open period.
   b. Many employees away from headquarters felt that their opinion
      would not matter, so why invest the time.
   c. Additionally, many of the nonheadquarters employees did not have
      an interest or have buy-in to take the survey.

Step 5: Develop a plan to close significant gaps.
Now that the actual problems have been discovered, leadership, working
side-by-side with representatives from the remote locations, begin to build
a plan to address the situation.
   To address challenge 1, Astro planned to:

■ Take iPads into the field and onto the rigs for employees to easily input
   their feedback, anonymously and without having to access a computer.
   This allowed the survey to be completed in real-time and with no
   challenges.
■ Organize group lunches for employees, where manager spoke
   of the importance of the survey and made available computer
   terminals, so employees could complete the survey privately
   after they had finished their free lunch. They also passed iPads
   around the room, allowing employees to take the survey quickly
   while still seated at the lunch tables. This allowed the employees
   to come together in a fun space, share a meal, and also complete the survey in a manner that felt most comfortable to each
   individual.

To address challenge 2, Astro implemented numerous initiatives including
the following:

■ Mr. Longhorn began a Management by Walking Around initiative where
   he would go to remote locations to meet the people who worked for
   him. By doing this, he begin to build a relationship beyond CEO/worker,
   humanizing headquarters and making workers more comfortable not
   only providing feedback but also more willing to share, because they felt
   their opinions mattered.

■ Videos were created showcasing Mr. Longhorn and leadership from the remote locations speaking directly to employees about what the survey was and how their input could affect the organization's strategic plan and goals for the upcoming year. By working hand-in-hand with familiar faces, Mr. Longhorn was building on the success of his Management by Walking Around initiative, deepening trust and engagement with all of his employees.

■ Additional videos were created and shared, demonstrating how change was implemented from previous years by showing before and after scenarios communicated by actual employees of the organization. Employees were shown exactly how their input had been used to make the organization a better place. By showing the positive change that came from past survey responses, employees saw that their voice did matter.

Employees responded so well to these strategies that the respondents increased over 50% in the following year. Mr. Longhorn was thrilled with the 50% increase, as well as the new connection he had built with his employees working away from headquarters.

By considering the company culture and structure, and the concerns of the employees not seeing the value in giving their input, the team succeeded!

6.5.5 Observation

Just like all of the previous methods for data collection, observation can be formal or informal. Informal observations are merely your personal views about what is happening (but informed by careful observation). Formal observations can be open-ended or close-ended, again, depending on the level of structure put to the engagement. As with the previously mentioned methods, close-ended observation will provide you with the most structure and the most definitive data, but steps need to be taken to ensure that your observation is properly planned and completed.

When using a close-ended observation as your data collection method, the first key is to know that you need to observe quantifiable behaviors. While getting a sense of the mood in the room is important information, it is not decision-quality data. Instead, you need to choose observable, measurable behaviors you can count and track. This will give you the data points needed when reporting findings and making next-step decisions in the planning stage of an OD intervention.

As the first step, you must take time to decide what behaviors you will watch for to gather data that can be linked to your planned decision criteria. Then, in thinking about the organization, you need to choose observation locations you think will enable you to see the behaviors for which you are looking. These can be real-time locations or simulated locations.

6.5.5.1 Real-Time Location Observation

Using real-time locations for observation is a great way to get a feel for what really happens in an organization. It is also difficult, sometimes, to get clients on board with observing real-time meetings. People fear that when observed, behaviors will be different because individuals will play to the OD professional, secrets will be compromised, or a multitude of other excuses.

In our experience, while a behavioral charade can be kept up for a short time, it is rarely sustainable (think 30 minutes or more). It has been our experience that people's true colors show through pretty quickly in observation situations. Usually it does not take long for the audience to forget that the OD practitioner is in the room. Especially in situations of stress, individuals often revert to their most comfortable state and behavioral observation succeeds.

When doing a behavioral observation, it is critical to use a well-developed behavioral observation form. Currently, you can find most examples of these forms related to children or schools, but with some adjustment, you can transform them into a working document for OD.

■ To create your form, be percise and purposeful as follows:
  a. Outline the exact behaviors for which you will be observing.
  b. Be as precise as possible.
  c. List observable, actionable behaviors, not just ideas or perceptions.
  d. Be sure you have drawn a link between the behavior you are measuring and the conclusion you can draw from the data you gather.
■ What should your form look like?
  a. The form you use when performing a behavioral observation needs to be simple, yet complete. Often, you have very little time to write long statements (because you should be spending most of your time observing behaviors).
  b. Write the behavior for which you are observing and leave space to indicate how many times you observe the behavior with check marks. In a group behavioral observation, be sure to leave space to

indicate a name or description of the individual who perpetuates the behavior. Even better if you can give each individual in the meeting a letter to represent them, so you merely have to write one character to represent each person.

■ Technology can help:

a. As technology advances, software is being created that can count behaviors in real time. Do not forget to tap into these technology resources as you develop your data collection plan.

For more information and help in this area, please refer to the worksheet at the end of this chapter to help you create a strong observational data collection.

Of course, if your client is against letting you quietly observe the team on the job, there are still ways to use observation as a method of data gathering.

6.5.5.2 Simulated Location Observation

If you cannot get clients to agree to real-time observation, another way to gather data through observation is to use technology or to observe a simulation. Individuals are sometimes more comfortable speaking out over teleconferences or on company discussion boards. Observation of these situations can often provide good data that can be used in OD engagements. Working clients through a simulation or case study and observing behaviors in this outside-of-the-daily-office-routine will provide data that can also be helpful. Taking groups to outdoor adventure sites (think ropes courses or the like) or putting them through an escape room experience (think real-life version of those addictive games you play on your smartphone like "Can You Escape") can also provide a great place for OD observation.

The important thing is that individuals know that they are being observed and evaluated, so they do not feel like they have been part of a "got'ya" sneak attack.

So again, let's take a step back and work thought a few short vignettes that discuss choosing observable behaviors and picking an observation location to collect relevant data, not just noise.

In observation 1, you have been tasked with creating a communication culture profile for your client.

You know that you will need to observe behaviors around the communication culture in the whole organization, so you decide that observing meetings will be one of the data-gathering methods you use. To get a picture of the entire organization, you know that you need to observe a set of senior leadership meetings, staff meetings, and mixed attendee meetings (so meetings where both senior leaders and staff are present).

By observing this range of meeting, you get a good view of how the levels of the organization communicate among peers, and how they communicate information in mixed groups. Looking at communication culture both between and among levels of the organization will allow you to form the full picture for which you are searching.

Once you line up your observation-meeting schedule, you need to decide what behaviors you wish to observe. For an OD question such as communication culture, your list should include behaviors such as:

- Who opens the meeting (individual's name)?
- Who talks during the meeting (individuals' names)?
- For how long do individuals speak uninterrupted?
- How often does each person talk?
- Who talks after whom (individuals' names)?
- Who interrupts others (individual's name)?
- How often are individuals interrupted?
- What body language is used during the discussion and by whom?
  - Examples: Crossed arms, leaning back in chain, checking cell phone, and so on.
- Who looks at whom when they talk (individuals' names)?
- Who supports what a speaker says (individual's name)?
- Who provides counter points to what a speaker says (individual's name)?

As we have said, the behaviors you track will differ depending on what OD engagement you are observing. Now, let's assume you are completing a close-ended observation to determine the decision-making culture of an organization.

In observation 2, you have been tasked with determining the decision-making culture of your client organization.

In the planning phase of the engagement, you have considered the organization's unique culture and determined that just observing meetings will not give you a full picture of the decision-making culture of this organization. You observe not only meetings, but also put individuals through a team simulation or case study exercise to take them out of their comfort zone and really see them in action.

You may use some of the behavior triggers above, but might also observe for some other important behaviors such as:

- How consensus is measured, a formal vote or other methods?
- How many options are proposed before a decision is made?
- Who proposes the options?
- Are options proposed formally (written) or informally (discussed)?
- Does the entire team need to agree?
- How many people speak their opinions before a decision is made?
- How long are individuals given to state their opinions before a decision is made?
- How often are individuals interrupted when starting their opinions?
- How often are commenters asked if they have finished stating their opinions before the discussion moves on?

Some other common behaviors you may observe for, depending on the situation, include the following:

- Consensus-testing behaviors
- Harmonizing behaviors
- Gatekeeping behaviors
- Encouraging behaviors
- Compromising behaviors
- Standard setting and testing behaviors
- Initiating behaviors
- Behaviors that lead to seeking information or opinions from others
- Giving information behaviors
- Clarifying or elaborating behaviors and/or
- Summarizing behaviors

See Table 6.8 for examples of what each of these behaviors can look like in the workplace.

So observations can get you lot of data when structured properly. For a summary, see Table 6.9.

6.5.6 Examination of Records

The last method we will discuss as it relates to the collection of data for an OD intervention is the examination of records. In an examination of records, the OD practitioner gathers data from printed or electronic material available

Table 6.8   Examples of Behaviors That Can Be Observed in the Workplace

Critical Behavior That Can Be Observed	What They Look Like in the Workplace
Consensus-testing behaviors	• Requesting feedback • Active listening (repeating what was heard after a speaker finishes talking) • Asking probing, directed questions
Harmonizing behaviors	• Asking for opinions from everyone • Checking in to ensure speakers have finished their thoughts before others start speaking • Asking if everyone feels they were heard
Gatekeeping behaviors	• Interrupting • Blocking access to individuals or groups • Not openly sharing information with the entire team • Avoiding questions with incomplete or misdirected answers
Encouraging behaviors	• Active listening (repeating what was heard after a speaker finishes talking) • Asking questions • Clarifying points before moving on
Compromising behaviors	• Asking if everyone is willing to move forward with the current plan • Asking if everyone is able to move forward with the current plan
Standard setting and testing behaviors	• Asking if everyone is clear on the role they play moving forward • Asking if everyone is clear on next steps • Asking for the group to repeat back the plan, as they understand it
Initiating behaviors	• Restating the meeting outcomes at the end of a meeting • Formally summarizing the meeting outcomes/next steps in written communication with the team • Checking-in (formally and/or informally) with team members after a plan is set in place
Behaviors that lead to seeking information or opinions from others	• Asking direct questions • Requiring that all members of a team speak • Calling on members of a team and specifically asking for their feedback
Giving information behaviors	• The presence of formal communication channels (e-mail, website, blogs, etc.) • Open door communication policies

(Continued)

Table 6.8 (*Continued*)   Examples of Behaviors That Can Be Observed in the Workplace

Critical Behavior That Can Be Observed	What They Look Like in the Workplace
Clarifying or elaborating behaviors	• Formal feedback discussions • Formal progress report discussions
Summarizing behaviors	• Spoken review of decisions and next steps • Written review of decisions and next steps

Table 6.9   Pros and Cons of Observation

Positives of Using Observation	Challenges of Using Observation
Gives the ability to gather deep data in real-time situations	Does not allow for immediate follow-up questions to clarify understanding
Allows you to examine nonverbal behavior and responses	People can change their behaviors when being observed
Gives you additional data allowing you to put meaning into context and explain outcomes	Observing individuals without permission can lead to ethical dilemmas
Opportunity to focus on the environment and take extensive notes, if needed	Advances in technology open new opportunities for observation, but can be expensive
Researcher blends into the situation over time without being a distraction	Time consuming

both from the company and though outside resources. Again, it is critical when using this method to be very intentional in the records you are collecting. When using this method, more than any other method, you can easily get distracted by noise.

Noise, in this context, relates to data you can gather that has no true impact on the overall success of failure of the particular OD intervention you are pursuing. Now, some may say that all data are relevant or you can never have too much data when deciding. We would like to ask you to reconsider these statements, and instead look at this method with a different lens. Ask

Table 6.10   Items to Use When Examining Records

Internal Company Records	External Records
Company strategic plan and action plans	Social media outlets
Personnel records	News
Internal websites and discussion boards	Organization reviews
Audits and inspections	Client reviews
Annual Employee Survey and results	External audits, inspections, and consumer reviews

Table 6.11   Pros and Cons of Examination of Records

Positives of Examination of Records	Challenges of Examination of Records
Can give you a deep understanding of organization structure, the foundation for any OD initiative	Sorting through the noise to determine what documents will provide you with relevant data
Official records, not opinions	Time consuming
Current data and numbers	Gaining full access and permission to records

yourself, "What question will I be able to answer once I have this data in my hand?" If the answer is "I don't know," you need to go back to the planning stage of the intervention and more clearly define your data collection to link to your intended outcomes. Even worse, if the answer is "there is no question this data will allow me to answer" than consider not collecting it.

When thinking about examination of records, there is a long list of recourses you can cull. Some are included in Table 6.10.

And like each of the methods we have discussed previously, examination of records has positives and challenges, as shown in Table 6.11.

6.6 Chapter Summary

As with anything, each of these methods has its own strengths and challenges. Therefore, a practitioner may use a mixed methods approach to maximize data-gathering potential. It is left to the discretion and experience of the researcher to decide what is best.

The best advice we can give for data collection is to go into each situation with a clear understanding that every piece of data you collect will take time and energy. Everything you collect will keep you from collecting something else. Use your plan to ensure you collect data that can be matched to a question; use the tips and tricks discussed here to ensure you are collecting decision-quality data, not just noise; and build your data collection plan to fit your OD initiative and the organization with which you are working.

Other key takeaways we hope to impart from this chapter include the following:

1. Data are only relevant when it is useful to your individual situation. Start data collection with a plan to ensure what you collect will be decision quality and actionable. If you cannot make a strong case for what decision the data will help you make, you should strongly reconsider spending time and energy collecting it.
2. Ensure that your data collection method(s) will allow you to collect data efficiently, objectively, completely, and accurately for your particular situation. Your method should also allow you enough flexibility to be successful, while collecting data that can be compared in order to help you make decisions.
3. All data collection methods have positives and challenges. By fully understanding your data needs and the power of each method, you will be able to build a successful data collection strategy.

6.7 Crafting a Strong Behavioral Observation Worksheet

Use the worksheet below to ensure you have created a through observation plan before using observation as a data collection method in an OD engagement.

Step 1: Mark in column 1 which indicators you will track.
Step 2: Indicate in column 2 what measure you will use for each (suggested measures are included on the worksheet).
Step 3: Indicate in column 3 what you plan to use this observational data to determine (suggested next steps are included on the worksheet).

Items I Will Track			
Hierarchy Indicators		**Measure**	**Next Step**
	Who opens the meeting	Name	Determine who the group leader is
	Who talks during the meeting	Name	Stratify group members into contributor buckets
	How often does each person talk	Count	Further stratify group members into top, moderate, and low contributors
	For how long do individuals speak uninterrupted	Minutes	Further stratify group members into top, moderate, and low contributors
	Who talks after whom	Names	Define the group structure
	Who interrupts others	Name and count	Determine individuals in need of group control
	How often are individuals interrupted	Count	Further define potential control issues
Body Language Indicators			
	Crossed arms	Name and count	Define the group mood
	Leaning back in chain	Name and count	Define the group mood
	Checking cell phone	Name and count	Define the group mood
Cohort Indicators			
	Who looks at whom when they talk	Names	Define subgroups inside of the group
	Who is participating in a side conversation	Names	Define subgroups inside of the group
	How often do side conversations occur	Count	Determine the strength of the subgroups inside of the group
	Who supports what a speaker says	Names and count	Determine subgroups' structure
	Who provides counter points to what a speaker says	Name and count	Determine the group's devil's advocate

(*Continued*)

Items I Will Track			
Cohort Indicators		**Measure**	**Next Step**
	How often are counter points stated	Count	Determine if the group is a victim of group think
	How long do individuals have when making counter points	Minutes	Determine if the group is a victim of group think
Consensus Indicators			
	How many formal votes are used	Count	Determine decision-making culture
	Who initiates the vote	Name	Define decision-making hierarchy
	How often does everyone need to approve for a vote to pass	Count	Define decision-making strategy
	How many options are proposed before a decision is made	Count	Define decision-making structure
	Who proposes the options	Name	Determine decision-making hierarchy
Style Indicators			
	How many opinions are proposed formally (in writing)	Count	Determine decision-making culture
	How many opinions are proposed informally (discussed)	Count	Determine decision-making culture
	What percentage of the team is engaged in a decision discussion	¼, ½, ¾	Define decision-making norms
	What percentage of the team is engaged in a decision vote	¼, ½, ¾	Define decision-making norms
	What percentage of the team is engaged in a decision execution	¼, ½, ¾	Define decision-making norms

(*Continued*)

Items I Will Track			
Style Indicators		**Measure**	**Next Step**
	How many times are people asked to speak their opinion before a decision is made	Count	Define decision-making culture
	Who asks for others to speak their opinion	Name	Determine decision-making hierarchy
	How many people speak with their opinions before a decision is made	Count	Define decision-making strategy
	How long are individuals given to state their opinions before a decision is made	Minutes	Define decision-making culture
	How often are individuals interrupted when starting their opinions	Count per speaker	Define decision-making culture
	How often are commenters asked if they have finished stating their opinions before the discussion moves on	Count	Define decision-making norms

Bibliography

Barnfield, H. (Ed.). 2014. *FYI for Your Improvement: Competencies Development Guide* (6th ed.). Los Angeles, CA: Korn Ferry.

Clark, R. E., and Estes, F. 2002. *Turning Research into Results. A Guide to Selecting The Right Performance Solutions.* Atlanta, GA: CEP Press.

Creswell, J. W. 2007. *Qualitative Inquiry and Research Design: Choosing among Five Approaches* (2rd ed.). Thousand Oaks, CA: Sage.

Creswell, J. W. 2013. *Research Design: Qualitative, Quantitative, and Mixed Methods Approaches.* Thousand Oaks, CA: Sage.

Eisenhardt, K. M. 1989. Building theories from case study research. *The Academy of Management Review*, 14, 532–550. Retrieved on September 29, 2016, from http://www.jstor.org/stable/258557.

Glesne, C. 2006. *Becoming Qualitative Researchers: An Introduction* (3rd ed.). Boston, MA: Pearson Education Inc.

Gupta, K., Sleezer, C. M., and Russ-Eft, D. F. 2007. *A Practical Guide to Needs Assessment* (2nd ed.). San Francisco, CA: Jossey-Bass.

Kezar, A. 2005. Consequences of radical change in governance: A grounded theory approach. *The Journal of Higher Education*, 76, 634–668. Retrieved on September 29, 2016, from http://www.jstor.org/stable/3838781.

Khan, S., and VanWynsberghe, R. 2008. Cultivating the under-mined: Cross-case analysis as knowledge mobilization. *Forum: Qualitative Social Research*, 9. Retrieved on September 29, 2016, from http://www.qualitative-research.net/index.php/fqs/article/viewArticle/334.

Kolb, J. 2011. *Small Group Facilitation: Improving Process and Performance in Groups and Teams*. Amherst, MA: HRD Press, Inc.

Miles, M. B., and Huberman, A. M. 1994. *Qualitative Data Analysis: An Expanded Sourcebook* (2nd ed.). Thousand Oaks, CA: Sage.

Patton, M. Q. 1997. *Utilization-focused evaluation: The new century text*. Thousand Oaks, CA: Sage.

Scannell, E. E., and Newstrom, J. W. 1994. *Games Trainers Play: Experiential Learning Exercises*. New York: McGraw-Hill, Inc.

Silberman, M. 2006. *Active Training: The handbook of Techniques, Designs, Case Examples, and Tips* (3rd ed.). San Francisco, CA: Pfeiffer.

Stake, R. 1995. *The Art of Case Study Research*. Thousand Oaks, CA: Sage.

Stake, R. 2006. *Multiple Case Study Analysis*. New York: Guildford Press.

Strauss, A., and Corbin, J. 1990. *Basics of Qualitative Research: Grounded Theory Procedures and Techniques*. London: Sage.

Strauss, A., and Corbin, J. 1998. *Basics of Qualitative Research: Techniques and Procedures for Developing Grounded Theory* (2nd ed.). London: Sage.

Yin, R. K. 1989. *Case Study Research: Design and Method* (1st ed.). Thousand Oaks, CA: Sage.

Yin, R. K. 2003. *Case Study Research: Design and Method* (3rd ed.). Thousand Oaks, CA: Sage.

Additional Online Resources

The authors would like to thank Angel McCormack (Sacramento, CA), for her help in building out the below list of resources.

There are many examples of OD surveys and OD interview guides available for your use. You can find many great resources at http://www.hr-survey.com/ including the following:

■ Employee opinion surveys – http://www.hr-survey.com/EmployeeOpinion.htm
■ Training needs assessment – http://www.hr-survey.com/TrainingNeeds.htm
■ HR audit surveys – http://www.hr-survey.com/HRAudit.htm

Additionally, there are numerous instruments that the OD practitioners can use when collecting data. Some great instruments include the following:

■ Korn Ferry Assessment of Leadership Potential: http://store.kornferry. com/store/lominger/en_US/pd/ThemeID.2815600/productID.315803300
■ Viaedge™ Learning Agility Assessment: http://store.kornferry.com/store/ lominger/en_US/DisplayCategoryProductListPage/ThemeID.2815600/ categoryID.19946100
■ *Voices®*, a web-enabled 360° feedback system: http://store.kornferry. com/store/lominger/en_US/pd/ThemeID.2815600/productID.127298200
■ DISC Personality Testing: http://discpersonalitytesting.com/
■ Myers Briggs Type Indicator (MBTI) free version (not the actual MBTI test, but very similar- takes about 10 minutes): http:// www.16personalities.com/free-personality-test
  − Once it generates the four-letter code (1 of 16 types), go to http://www. personalitypage.com/html/portraits.html and http://personalityjunkie. com/more-type-profiles
■ Free Keirsey Temperament Sorter®-II (KTS®-II): http://www.keirsey. com/sorter/register.aspx
  − Takers will be one of four that should coincide with their MBTI type
■ The Big Five Project: www.outofservice.com/bigfive
  − Measures the "big five" personality characteristics: openness, conscientiousness, extraversion, agreeableness, and neuroticism
■ Learnmyself: http://www.seemypersonality.com/#q1
  − Another free personality test that correlates well with MBTI and breaks it down a little further
■ Strengthsfinder: http://shop.gallup.com/strengths/1595620117-428.html
  − Ranks top five strengths of 34. You can purchase and take the assessment for $9.99 online. The top five in order are unique to each person and only one in 33 million people will have those five in that particular order!

You can also find a curated collection of free and open tools that can help you in learning about the creation and use of data gathering tools and techniques at www.merlot.org and www.youtube.com.

Chapter 7

Feeding Back Data and Action Planning for Organization Development

Angela L.M. Stopper and Julie D. Staggs

Contents

7.1 Introduction

Continuing our discussion, we have navigated through the basic concepts of organization development (OD) diagnosis and assessment, models to utilize, planning needed to properly and successfully engage, and the tools and techniques to collect and analyze data into meaningful and actionable information that can be used in a successful OD engagement. This chapter will focus on the next step, how to provide feedback in a meaningful manner that includes insight, leads your client to draw actionable recommendations, and builds a strong base for action planning and implementation (launch) of the agreed upon recommendations.

Presenting feedback begins with understanding the purpose and goal of the initiative, and understanding your stakeholders' perspectives. The key is to focus on aligning the feedback with the client's goals in mind, and then providing and presenting the outcomes and insights of your data collected in a relevant, understandable, professional, and actionable way. While this seems logical and simple, it is not so easy to do and involves several considerations and logistical steps. Key issues in feeding back data and action planning include getting buy-in at all levels through joint action planning, determining ownership and accountability for action items, and intentionally considering and planning for change management for successful implementation.

In this chapter, we will discuss how to plan, develop, and deliver impactful feedback, work with stakeholder groups to jointly develop an action plan, and position for successful implementation by looking at the who, what, and how for both feedback and action planning.

7.2 What Is Feedback?

Let's begin by providing a working definition of feedback. Feedback is the process of informing the client and key stakeholders about the results of the assessment process. Feedback is necessary for a consultant and client to achieve a common understanding of an organization's current condition, so that they can work to identify the needed change.

When giving feedback, it is important to ensure that you give feedback that is limited, descriptive, verifiable, impactful, and un-finalized. Some keys to doing this are included in Table 7.1.

7.3 Planning

The overall feedback plan and agenda should be focused around providing enough data, so that you and your client can answer *what, how, when, and who* as they relate to the stated initiative.

Table 7.1 Key Elements of Giving Strong Feedback and Examples of Each

Key Elements of Giving Strong Feedback	Examples of How to Accomplish This
Limited	• Give feedback in short, digestible segments • Mix positive and negative feedback into every discussion • Check in for understanding
Descriptive	• Be specific • Do not make assumptions of intent • Do not attack
Verifiable	• Use real-life examples • Use data • Bring in quotes from others
Impactful	• Link action and ramification • Paint a picture for future success • Use personal or other tangible examples
Un-finalized	• Leave room for discussion • Allow time for response • Discuss options and create the path to improvement

- What:
  - What is the problem?
- How:
  - What is the solution to the problem and why is this solution the best compared to other solutions?
  - How should the solution be implemented, and how much will the solution cost (budget)?
- When:
  - What is the timeline for the solution?
- Who:
  - Who is responsible, who is engaged, and why are they important (staffing)?

As you work through the organization assessment and arrive at the time to provide feedback, careful planning is essential. Whether you are an internal or an external consultant, determining each stakeholder group to whom you will be providing feedback, what they need to hear, how the information must be presented, and when they will receive it are to be considered. Though eventually all within the organization should be involved, sharing the feedback from the assessment may only include certain stakeholders or portions of certain stakeholder groups at certain times.

7.4 Feedback Delivery Planning

Often, there is a workgroup or task force who may comprise senior leaders and those who will lead the implementation of the initiative (launch). This group's composition may be planned to represent the organization (including participants from various levels and functions of the organization) or the composition of the group may be more politically designed for the best buy-in and implementation success. Typically, this is the group with which you should provide feedback first.

Beyond the workgroup, multiple stakeholders will be interested in the outcome and feedback from the assessment. These stakeholder groups include senior leaders, managers, individual contributors, and clients of the organization. Identifying and then better understanding the profile of each stakeholder group assists you in determining how to focus the insights and findings of the feedback to be most relevant and compelling to each stakeholder group.

For each group, you should outline the group's function, focus, and goals either during the assessment process or as part of planning for feedback. Understanding how the group fits into the organization, their interdependences, and their role and responsibility as part of the overall corporate strategy will aid you in determining how to best present your findings to the group. Addressing their presenting problems and highlighting the findings of the assessment in a way most relevant to each stakeholder group will prepare them to take ownership of the action steps needed as you move into implementation.

7.4.1 What

Having identified each stakeholder group, you will want to contextualize your feedback based on the focus and role of the group in alignment with and in support of the overall strategy of the organization. Without this alignment, any one group may not understand why they may need to take action or how they relate to the whole. Providing relevant and meaningful feedback is critical to getting buy-in, commitment, and action that fills gaps and moves the organization forward.

7.4.2 How

Two key variables come into consideration when looking at how you will provide feedback to each stakeholder group—format and setting. The format may be in a report for individuals to review and absorb individually or in a presentation where they will hear and interact with the information live as a group. The setting can be individual or group, whichever you feel will allow you the best opportunity to socialize the information while preparing stakeholders for action planning.

In this step, it is critical to share information that can lead the group to a solution, and provide enough context in order to allow the group to compare and contrast different solutions to come up with the best. It is also important to share budget-relevant information. If the best solution comes with the biggest price tag, the group needs to hear and understand that in the feedback session.

7.4.3 When

As part of the timeline, you as the consultant must first define the feedback delivery order. Properly ordering your feedback delivery to stakeholder groups cascades the information through the organization and helps you to gather feedback as you go. This is critical (politically), as taking this inward view through the assessment process can uncover areas of weakness and opportunity. Being sensitive to the possible perceptions of different groups once they receive the feedback will aid in the acceptance of the information and is a way to drive action.

7.4.4 Who: Identifying Organizational Strategy and Goals

When planning a feedback session, having a solid grasp of the organization's strategy and goals will serve you well and should be used as your overarching organizing factor. Although you may find the presenting problem to be different at various points in the organization, having this highest level reference point will anchor the feedback to each stakeholder group and provide a connection between their potentially differing presenting problems. Aligning the divisions' and functions' presenting problems and goals to the overall organization will provide a more streamlined action plan.

7.4.5 Who: Identifying Stakeholders

Whether feedback is initially presented to all stakeholder groups or subsets, defining the groups and articulating the profile of each will be helpful for you to understand the findings. Analysis of the data typically has highlighted where opportunities lie, and by identifying all the groups, you can be well positioned to determine and help assign action steps, which will move the organization to success. Considering variables such as function, focus, goals, positioning, interactions, and inter-relationships with others in the organization is the key. By knowing all of this information about each stakeholder group, you can more suitably provide feedback to align the stakeholder group with the findings, the overall organization, and meaningful action steps to create change with impact.

7.5 Feedback Planning: Format

Whether providing information in a report or presentation, the *format* of feedback should follow a logical and consistent order for all stakeholder groups. Providing the high-level presenting problem for context sets the stage for the findings. Following this, we suggest the following order:

- Presenting problem
- Assessment process overview
- Executive summary of findings and insights
- Details of specific findings and insights
- Guidance to a solution set
- Appendices of data

Using this logical order, it is easy to provide full information, and through good design, stakeholders can more fully understand the information relevant to their group and how they fit within the whole organization.

7.5.1 Presenting Problem

Stating the presenting problem acknowledges the challenge articulated by the stakeholder group. This is a point of beginning, though it may prove inaccurate based on the findings from the assessment process. With the perceived problem and then the validated problem both visible in the presentation, a much nicer dialog may take place to best determine the accurate problem through action planning.

7.5.2 Assessment Process Overview

Outlining the steps that were taken in the assessment informs the stakeholder groups about the components of the process that were designed and executed to better understand the organization. This information should include steps to inform the group of who was involved, how the data were gathered, and where each stakeholder group was represented.

A sample of what the assessment process overview can look like is represented in Figures 7.1 and 7.2.

7.5.3 Executive Summary of Findings/Insights

Prior to going deeply into the findings and insights of an initiative, a summary provides key themes and overall information to prepare the group members to better receive and digest the details. This concise summary

Overview of methodology

For this engagement, we collected, reviewed, and integrated information from the sources below to make observations, draw conclusions, and provide recommendations:

✓ Initial discussions and working session with OrgX executive team members

✓ Review of strategy documents, division plans, OrgX structure documents, recent OrgX-surveys (employee and client)

✓ Structured interviews with designated leaders, managers, and individual contributors of OrgX (16 interviewees)

✓ Focus groups with division leadership, managers, independent contributors, and clients (53 total participants)

✓ Online survey distributed to all OrgX employees with 540 responses

Figure 7.1 Often, outlining the assessment process steps in words is necessary in order to gain the needed buy-in from stakeholders groups you wish to reach during a feedback session.

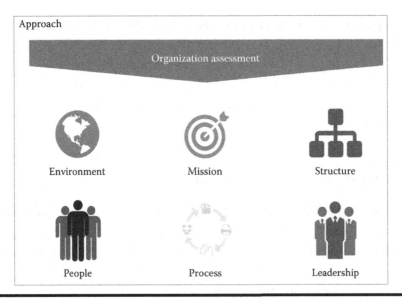

Figure 7.2 In addition to words, pictures can help to really build an understanding of the process that was undertaken. We recommend you to use both in your feedback sessions in order to make a strong impact.

provides talking points for the group members to use, as they help to socialize and spread the information that will ultimately drive the action steps and overall changes.

Some sample slides that can be used in an executive summary are shown in Figures 7.3 through 7.5.

Executive summary

• Study identified a critical need for near- and long-term strategy definition

• Findings point toward a strong desire and readiness for change

• Immediate needs for direction-setting and action are as follows:

  • Set clear goals

  • Increase communication and transparency

  • Manage the change

• Importance for new dean to articulate and drive the vision and strategy

• Fundamental areas of concern include: leadership effectiveness, decision-making, accountability (or lack thereof), climate derailers, excess programming, and staffing imbalances

• Roles, reporting relationships, and overall direction are widely unclear

• Articulated concern regarding the speed at which the School can make necessary changes

• Many who participated in this study expressed a commitment to the School and offered support in "righting the ship"

This report outlines the actions that will lay the foundation for a new strategic direction.

Figure 7.3   Use an executive summary to prepare the group for the meet of the findings. This is a great place to include the talking points you want the stakeholder group to take away from the feedback session and share through the organization.

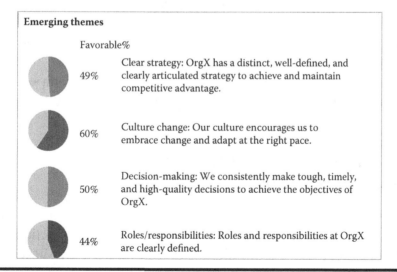

Emerging themes

Favorable%

49% Clear strategy: OrgX has a distinct, well-defined, and clearly articulated strategy to achieve and maintain competitive advantage.

60% Culture change: Our culture encourages us to embrace change and adapt at the right pace.

50% Decision-making: We consistently make tough, timely, and high-quality decisions to achieve the objectives of OrgX.

44% Roles/responsibilities: Roles and responsibilities at OrgX are clearly defined.

Figure 7.4   Again, mixing pictures with words really makes for broad appeal. When you can incorporate easily understandable charts and graphs into your executive summary, do so. It will go far in helping to tell the story you need to share with the feedback.

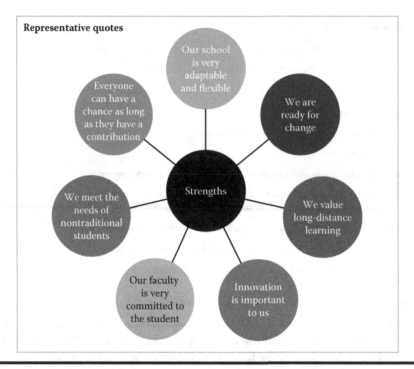

Figure 7.5   It is always important to use direct quotes when delivering OD feedback. It goes a long way in showing the audience that you are not there to tell them what to do. Instead, you are there to share findings and help them to build an action plan.

7.5.4 Specific Findings/Insights Details

To support and illuminate each of the findings and your insights, more detail should be provided for each of the key findings. To do so, select the best presentation and ensure that you are specific, clear, compelling, and impactful. This can take many forms from simple text to illustrative graphics. See Figures 7.6 and 7.7 for examples.

7.5.5 Guidance of Practitioners to a Solution or Set of Solutions

In this section of the feedback process, it is important to share findings and insights that will begin to lead the stakeholder groups to an action plan on how to best deal with the findings. This can be done by showing the findings in buckets such as urgent, needs immediate action, important, and so on. Remember, OD consulting is not management consulting. You are not tasked with going into the organization and delivering the solution. Instead, you are tasked with leading the group to their own solution.

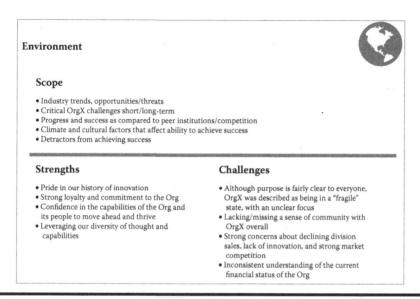

Figure 7.6   This slide shows specific finding detail using only words. When creating detail slides, be sure the information is visually appealing and not too overwhelming, or you will lose your audience.

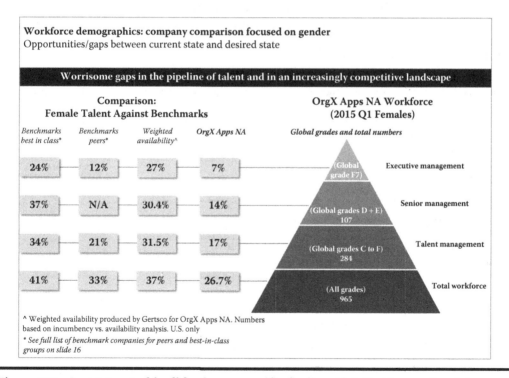

Figure 7.7   In contrast, this slide shows specific findings detailed in mostly pictures. Use your best judgment, and mix both words and image slides to best represent the data you wish to share.

As we have said before, this requires strong facilitation skills as well as a client who understands the difference between management consulting and OD consulting. If you have a client who is looking for an "expert with all of the answers," you might want to reconsider taking on the initiative in the first place.

7.5.6 Appendices of Data

Considering the communication styles and desire to see support data for the findings and recommendations, it is helpful to use appendices at the end of a report or presentation to be best prepared to answer questions and support recommendations for action. Use this space to hold all of the data you gathered, in order to answer questions that come up during the feedback session. See Figure 7.8 for example.

7.6 Feedback Planning: Design

Assessment is worthless if it does not position the organization to reach agreement on the issues/problems, solutions, measurable change objectives,

2014 engagement survey: gender comparisons only

As found in the 2014 Apps NA Engagement Survey Report, both males and females responded equally favorable along most dimensions – learning and development, professional growth and development, and performance management.

Females did, however, respond less favorably along the following items (statistical significance among differences is not known). This may indicate some themes worth exploring further, such as trust and integrity, motivation, and diversity and inclusion.

THEMES IDENTIFIED BY KORN FERRY	ITEM AND DIMENSION	% OF FEMALES FAVORABLE (MALES)
Development and advancement	"I am knowledgeable about the OrgX competency and career framework for my role and grade."	60% (64%)
New hire onboarding	"OrgX integrates new colleagues into the company very well."	45% (52%)
Motivation	"The senior leadership of the OrgX Group (the CEO and the top leadership team) has communicated a vision of the future that motivates me."	51% (58%)
	"I feel I work for a company whole brand is strong in the marketplace."	55% (61%)
	"I would recommend OrgX as a place to work to a friend or colleague."	69% (74%)
Trust and integrity	"I trust the OrgX group senior leadership (the CEO and the top leadership team)."	58% (68%)
	"I feel that we live up to the group's value trust."	72% (78%)
	"I feel that we live up to the group's value honesty."	69% (78%)
Diversity and inclusion	I feel my manager/business unit actively promotes diversity and inclusion (providing equal career opportunities and respecting diversity differences).	73% (77%)

Figure 7.8 Any information that you do not have room for in the presentation, but that you feel is important should be stored as an appendix. This information can provide additional support to help you answer questions that arise during any feedback session.

and metrics by which to measure successful implementation. When designing your feedback, keep these indicators paramount. In fact, we suggest running your final deliverable by a friend or colleague and asking him or her the following questions after the presentation. If your colleague is unable to answer, you need to spend more time developing your feedback presentation.

- What presented information will you use to reach agreement on the issues in this organization?
- What presented information can you use to come to a list of actionable solutions to the issue?
- What information is presented that will allow you to weigh the positives and negatives of each solution in order to choose the ideal?
- What information is presented that will allow you to define the measurable change objectives needed to be outlined in moving from the current to the future state?
- What items can this company use as metrics by which to measure successful implementation of the action plan?

To best communicate the information found in the assessment phase of an OD initiative, it is helpful to use good design. A key to remember: Less is More. Selecting the few critical points and making them logical, relevant, connected, and clear are no small task. Many theories of presentation style and length exist with a common theme of presenting as concisely as possible with a story used to tie the information together. Remembering several communication styles and how individuals like to take in information will go far in highlighting important information and helping your audience to digest the information in a way to drive action. Several design options aligned with how they may best communicate information are listed in Table 7.2.

Table 7.2   Design Elements for Recommended Information Types

Design Element	Recommended Information Type
Prose	• Use key points and quotes
Graphics	• Charts and graphs make sense of a lot of data or complex data and data interactions
Bulleted lists	• Multiple points of information
Appendices	• Sample instruments or data • Space for detailed data to support findings, insights, and suggested action steps

7.7 Feedback Planning: Delivery and Facilitation Skills

7.7.1 Delivery Considerations

Another part of planning is determining if the feedback will be delivered one-on-one or in a group. You also need to decide what media you will use for feeding back assessment information. Table 7.3 lists suggested media, and some positives and negatives of each.

With the suggested components of design, it is necessary to be well versed in the social and communication styles of many individuals. This will help you to understand how best your stakeholders take in information and the best ways to connect, whether it may be through bullet points, stories, full data in spreadsheets, or just through reading and processing your findings.

Using knowledge of communication styles prior to your delivery will help you to communicate effectively and with impact. Based on this knowledge, designing slides considering the information to be communicated on each slide and varying the designs to appeal to multiple styles are the keys.

Along with designing the presentation with variety, being prepared with ample knowledge behind the slides, confident in your delivery of information, and prepared for questions can round out an impressive and effective feedback session. Checking in often with the audience to make sure they are tracking with you and clarifying any information they may question keep you in control of the pace and discussion, while enabling you to better understand how well you are communicating the desired information.

7.7.2 Facilitation Skills

Facilitation skills differ from delivery skills and involve having prepared open-ended questions to initiate and engage group members in discussion that provides their point of view, level of acceptance, and engagement with the findings.

It is important to remember that being a facilitator is different than being a discussion contributor. When facilitating, it is critical that you remain neutral.

Good facilitation includes the following:

■ Designing
■ Planning

Table 7.3 Media That Can Be Used in Feeding Back Assessment Data

Media	Positives	Challenges
Executive meetings	• Intimate, allows for questions and discussion • Allows for needed engagement at this level	• Time consuming • Can be seen by some as elitist or separating
Town hall meetings	• Quickly gets the word to the masses • Cost-effective way to communicate with large groups	• Room for misunderstanding, miscommunicaiton, and disengagement because of the large scale • Logistical hassles of arranging large group meetings
Unit level meeting	• Allows for unit-level discussion • Impactful in that communication can be customized to include "what's in it for me" at a unit level	• Can cause misgivings about speaking up in a room of only peers • Can lead to group think
One-on-One meetings	• Intimate, allows for questions and discussion • Completely customizable to include "what's in it for me" discussions	• Time consuming • Can be seen by some as elitist or separating
Videos	• Can be cost effective • Because of distribution technology, not time- or location-sensitive	• Becomes dated overtime • Takes special skills to engage through video • No immediate interaction
Video Conferencing	• Cost effective • Not location-sensitive	• Takes special skills to engage through video • Possible bandwith and technology issues
Websites	• Can be cost effective • Can capitalize on already available company resources	• Requires time and skill to create and maintain • Strategy and resources need to quickly deal with broken links and public complaints
Social media campaigns	• Engaging way to connect to workers (especially younger workers) • Quick way to spread both text and video information	• Requires time and skill to create and maintain • When poorly done, can create more issues than are solved (miscommunication, rabbit-holing, and rumor spreading)

- ◼ Guiding
- ◼ Controlling

Involving folks in the discussion enriches the feedback and insight of the facilitator and encourages engagement and buy-in of the key stakeholders. Also, listening and capturing the discussion whether on a flipchart, by audio-recording, or note-taking are important to facilitation. This helps you to then synthesize the feedback from stakeholder groups to utilize when designing an action plan and launch schedule.

While it is beyond the scope of this chapter to create the facilitator in you, we would like to connect you with a resource that can just do that. Please visit mindtools.com for a great discussion and tools on how to build facilitation skill: https://www.mindtools.com/pages/article/RoleofAFacilitator.htm

7.8 Action Planning

Now that you have planned and delivered feedback to stakeholder groups and facilitated discussions to gather feedback, you are ready to do action planning. In OD, action planning is the process of systematically planning a change effort using sound change models and principles. Gaining buy-in and commitment, and making this a joint process with the work group who will lead the implementation of the changes are critical to this step. The OD action-planning process includes the following four key steps:

- ◼ Determine the client's degree of choice about change (how much control do clients have in deciding whether to change and how to change?)
- ◼ Determine what needs to be changed
- ◼ Determine where to intervene
- ◼ Choose intervention technologies

Critical components to keep in mind when developing a process plan include the following:

- ◼ Ensuring that activities in the plan are clearly linked to the goals and priorities of the identified change
- ◼ Ensuring that activities are clearly identified as actionable and measurable rather than broadly generalized
- ◼ Linking and time sequencing discrete activities in order to show a road map from start to finish

- Planning for the unexpected by creating contingency plans
- Ensuring top management support and buy-in for the plan
- Ensuring that the plan includes metrics and accountability checkpoints, which will make it measurable
- Formalizing and gaining approval for the budget, ensuring that the plan will remain adequately funded throughout its life

This process includes several steps:

- Synthesizing data, insights, and feedback
- Defining success and determining metrics to measure it in alignment with organization strategy and goals
- Identifying priority action items
- Determining responsibilities and accountabilities for each action item
- Creating a timeline with status updates and review
- Engaging buy-in at all levels and
- Securing commitments at all levels

This process can take a single session or may involve several sessions to refine the entire plan to be ready for implementation. It is helpful to plan status updates and reviews, and to monitor interim goals to ascertain that progress and course are correct. The most effective action plans are organic and continue to evolve as implementation begins and continues.

But in general, there are a few key things to keep in mind. When creating an OD action plan, involvement of the key stakeholders in the planning process is critical. It is also necessary to evaluate who is in the best position to influence or contribute to the planning, implementation, and management of the effort and to decide who should be directly or indirectly involved in the planning process. This is often done by appointing a Change Agent, Change Champion, or a combination of both with clear roles established in order to lead the change project and form a Change Team, which is then tasked with clear planning and management roles in the change process.

It is also critical to remember to evaluate data relevant to the needed changes focusing on both the present conditions and the future ideal state. Evaluate the realities that must be considered in making needed changes such as readiness for change, support for change, and time and resources available for change. Everyone needs to agree on what is to be changed or improved—both the focus (whole or partial organizational change) and the level (transformational, fine-tuning, or somewhere in between).

It is also important to incorporate a system into your plan which will evaluate the effect of the initiative from a system's perspective by considering the impact that the change will have on the organization and the organization on the change. Explore ways to improve alignment between the change and organization, and agree on what is to be changed or improved based on what the decision-makers can and are willing to do.

As with anything, change is not easy, and a key success factor deals with identifying any forces working for and against the desired change that should be considered in developing a change strategy. This may include the exploration of intervention alternatives and creation of contingency plans.

As discussed in earlier chapters, the development of an action plan that is based on a sound change model and sound change principles will help to create a successful environment in which you can work. Again, having a plan in place to monitor and manage the change process with built-in feedback mechanisms to monitor progress is essential.

After a plan is created, use the following questions to ensure that the plan includes all of the necessary pieces to be successful. Does the plan address:

- Who should do what to make the change work?
- What needs to happen?
- In what order do steps need to happen?
- When should each step in the change process begin and end?
- Where should you see change occurring?
- Why is the change being made?
- How should the change process unfold?

All of these steps will increase the probability of completing a successful change effort.

7.9 Implementation: Pre-Launch and Launch

Once the action plan has been created with a timeline and responsibilities, the implementation can begin. Few processes are more intriguing in OD than assessment and action planning, and few processes can stimulate and result in more change. In the last stages of the initiative, known as pre-launch and launch, valuable information is gathered and analyzed, and a collaborative approach is used to evaluate the information and planned actions that provide a sound strategy for making organizations, groups, or individuals successful.

Implementation takes careful planning with attention to the reality of action plans and therefore change management considerations and steps should be put in place. Let us look at each phase individually.

7.9.1 Pre-Launch

Pre-launch begins when a consultant clearly has a client with a desire to start the hard work needed in an OD initiative and after the activities associated with marketing the plan, selling the plan, and gaining necessary buy-in have been completed. It concludes when the consultant and client have clarified the nature of the change effort, their working relationships, their expectations, and the contract.

Pre-launch is all about entering the organization, building the platform for engaging in change to work with the client, and contracting for that work. Because it builds the base on which the change initiative rests, the activities of the pre-launch phase are critical in successful OD work. As with any building, the quality of the foundation can set you up for success or failure, so pay careful attention to this step. At this stage, it is imperative that you look for red flags, such as the following:

- Lack of support in the organization
- Managers and employees who feel vulnerable
- Differing and biased perspectives about what is working, what is not working, and what needs to be done
- More "unknowns" than "knowns"
- Mixed motives for seeking a consultant's help (desire to change, financial trouble, need for a scapegoat, etc.)
- A past history of bad change experiences

These challenges and more are discussed in detail in our next chapter, but we would be remiss if we did not also mention them here.

7.9.2 Launch

In the launch phase of an OD engagement, all of your hard work is put into action. Action plans are implemented, and strategies are developed and executed to move the client organization to their most ideal future state.

Systems that you have planned for that will manage and monitor the change are enacted and accountabilities are engaged. Data, stories, and other valuable information are gathered in order to be shared so the organization stays engaged with the change effort as it moves forward.

Because action plans most often include change, and change is scary and hard, it is helpful to create launch phases with different timeframes to address short, medium, and long-term goals. Phases also allow for a cadence of reviews and opportunities to celebrate success intermittently rather than waiting for a year end or worse yet, the end of the initiative (which we know can take years). Phases also help build momentum and engagement with great visibility of progress in shorter timeframes.

And in the end, to successfully execute an action plan coming out of an organization assessment, a thoughtful and inclusive change management plan should be included in implementation. Key components include the following:

■ Senior leader champion and exemplar
■ Communications plan—internal and external with timeline
■ On-going feedback process
■ Plans and goals in context, at all levels, including groups and individuals

While this list of components seems simple, it is not easy to procure. Even so, we encourage you to create the change plan with great intention and live it out with focus.

7.10 Chapter Summary

Planning, preparing, and delivering feedback takes intentional focus and time. Jointly, creating an action plan with those charged with leading the implementation creates great buy-in and engagement. All of this extends the time needed to execute implementation, but should not be overlooked or skipped because of time worries. Positioning for success in executing action plans based on the organization assessment can yield great success and efficiency if planned, designed, and executed well. The key is focusing on infusing change management components and practices into the organization in which you are working and staying committed to the process.

7.11 The Feedback and Action-Planning Worksheet

When planning, have you considered:

Overall Feedback Plan and Agenda		
Who, What, How, When		
	Identify groups and individuals	
	Determine focus and message for each stakeholder in alignment with their part of the organization strategy and goals	
	Provide medium—presentation or report	
	Prioritize and schedule in meaningful and intentional order	
	Determine focus and message for each stakeholder in alignment with their part of the organization strategy and goals	
Identify Organization Strategy and Goals		
Overall Organization		
	Organization strategic plan	
	Division/Unit Goals	
	Presenting Problem	
Identify Stakeholders		
Identify for each stakeholder group—Senior Leaders/Managers/Individual Contributors/Clients		
	Functional focus	
	Goals	
	Relationship to organization strategy and goals	
	Presenting Problem	
	Interactions/inter-relationships within organization	
	Relevance of assessment findings	
Determine Feedback Mode—Presentation or Report		
Format		
	Presenting Problem	
	Assessment process overview	
	Executive overview of findings/insights	
	Specific findings/insights details	
	Guidance to a solution set	
	Appendices of data	
Design		
	Prose/Quotes	
	Graphics—charts and graphs	
	Bulleted lists	
	Appendices-sample instrument	
	Appendices of data	

For delivery, have you:

Delivery and Facilitation Skills		
Individual and/or Group		
	Consider communication styles of your audiences	
	Developed well-designed slides	
	Prepared findings and key discussion questions	
	Practiced executive presence and honed yourdelivery skills	
	Developed tools to have you solicit feedback with key questions	
	Prepped for a facilitated discussion	
	Left time to check in frequently for understanding and questions	
	Engaged tools to help capture discussion (audio/flip charts/note taking)	

For action planning, have you:

Action Plan Creation
Completed joint planning with work/implementation team
Synthesize data, insight and feedback
Define success and determine metrics to measure in alignment with organization strategy and goals
Identify and prioritize action items
Determine responsibilities and accountabilities for each action item
Create timeline
Engage buy-in at all levels
Secure commitment at all levels
Implementation
Written the plan to be utilized by work/implementation team
Divide action items and timeline into phases
Articulate, confirm and communicate roles and responsibilities
Create change management plan
Change Management
Included the following components
Senior leadership champion and exemplar
Communication plan—internal and external with timeline
Feedback process
Plans and goals in context at all levels including both group and individual

Bibliography

Bruce, R., and Wyman, S. 1998. *Changing Organizations, Practicing Action Training and Research*. Thousand Oaks, CA: Sage Publications, Inc.

Kotter, J. P. 1995. Leading change: Why transformation efforts fail. (cover story). *Harvard Business Review*, 73(2), 59–67.

Kotter, J. P. 1996. *Leading Change*. Boston, MA: Harvard Business Review Press.

Merrill, D. W., and Reid, R. H. 1981. *Personal Styles and Effective Performance: Making Your Style Work for You*. Radnor, PA: Chilton Book Company.

Rothwell, W. J., Stavros, J. M., Sullivan, R. L., and Sullivan, A. (eds.). 2010. *Practicing Organization Development: A Guide for Leading Change* (3rd ed.). San Francisco, CA: Pfeiffer.

Spector, B. 2013. *Implementing Organizational Change: Theory and Practice* (3rd ed.). Upper Saddle River, NJ: Pearson.

Taylor, P. 2005. *7-Slide Solution: Telling Your Business Story in seven Slides or Less*. Westport, CT: Silvermine Press.

Additional Online Resources

Use free online learning management system (LMS) tools like Canvas to create program sites for initiatives to share information, manage project communications and insight collaboration: https://canvas.instructure.com/login

Other online engagement tools include the following:

- ■ Blogging, creating personal pages
  - Edublogs—edublogs.org
  - Wordpress—wordpress.com
  - Twitter Microblogs—twitter.com
  - Glogster—http://www.glogster.com/
  - Weebly—http://www.weebly.com/
  - Padlet—http://padlet.com/
- ■ Collaborative writing
  - Etherpad/TitanPad—etherpad.com; titanpad.com
  - Google Docs—drive.google.com
  - Twiddla—twiddla.com
  - Wikispaces—wikispaces.com
- ■ Content maps
  - Cmap tools—http://ftp.ihmc.us
  - Lucid Chart—lucidchat.com
  - Mindmeister—mindmeister.com
- ■ Discussions
  - Piazza—piazza.com
  - Prulu—prulu.com
  - Voicethread—voicethread.com
- ■ Interactive media
  - Thinglink—thinglink.com
  - Zaption—zaption.com
- ■ Presentations
  - Prezi—orezi.com
  - Sliderocket—sliderocket.com
  - Slideshare—slideshare.net
  - Visual.ly
- ■ Screen capture/Sharing
  - Camtasia—techsmith.com/camtasia.html
  - Jing—techsmith.com/jing.html
  - Walkme—walkme.com
  - Screencastomatic—http://www.screencast-o-matic.com/
- ■ Storytelling
  - Storify—storify.com
- ■ Content creation
  - Paper.li

- – Surfmark—surfmark.com
- – Flickrpoet—http://www.storiesinflight.com/flickrpoet/
- – Zoho notebook—notebook.zoho.com
- ■ Timelines
  - – Dipity
- ■ Sharing recordings
  - – Audioboo.fm—http://audioboo.fm/
  - – Chirbit—http://www.chirbit.com/
- ■ Voice eLearning
  - – Voxopop—http://www.voxopop.com/
- ■ Online meetings
  - – Join Me—https://join.me/
  - – Adobe Connect—adobe.com/products/adobeconnect.html
  - – Google + Hangouts—plus.google.com
  - – Skype—skype.com

Chapter 8

Challenges and Their Related Opportunities in Diagnosis and Assessment for Organization Development

Angela L.M. Stopper

Contents

8.1 Introduction

Now that we have defined the steps needed in proper organizational diagnosis and assessment, shared some tools and models you can use, and shared strategies for collecting, analyzing, and feeding back data as part of the process, we would like to challenge you to think about ways that the process can go wrong.

Experience tells us that as human beings, we like to think that all undertakings we participate in will succeed. Never do we start a project thinking this time will be the time we fail. But if we are all honest, we can admit that not every initiative undertaken by an organization succeeds. Success can be even more elusive when you think about change and change leadership. As optimistic as humans are when looking to the future, we can be equally skeptical, dare I say afraid, of change.

So, if you go into an organizational diagnosis and assessment project with blinders on, thinking that everyone will engage fully and everything will progress perfectly, you are sure to be disappointed. Instead, you need to have thought deeply about the roadblocks you can come up against and plan for ways to chart an alternate route when those road blocks appear.

To do so, let's first explore some of the potential challenges that may arise when performing an organizational diagnosis and assessment. We will explore each step of the process and the challenges that can arise through some short vignettes.

8.2 Challenges That Can Arise in Planning for Assessment and Feedback

Jennifer has been assigned to lead a team-building engagement within her company, one of the best known brands in the wine industry. As a California native and devout wine drinker, she is excited to get out of the HR office and really get in touch with the individuals in her organization.

To prepare for the project, Jennifer puts what she knows about the company in order. Three months ago, the company hired its first nonfamily CEO. Shortly after being hired, the CEO announced that it was time to bring the "stuffy old company" into modern times. He has hired a new Winemaker and a new Director of Marketing to expand the company's reach into new markets. In doing so, they have announced that they will expand the product portfolio of the company to include sweeter wines and have even explored the use of screw top closures to replace the natural cork closures that the company has historically used.

Many employees at the company, including Jennifer, are aghast. How could such a prestigious old-family winery forsake its roots like this?

As Jennifer plans her team-building initiative, she cannot seem to get the disappointment she feels in the company's new direction out of her head. She looks at numerous opinion pieces in the trade magazines that support her dislike of sweet wines. She talks with others who agree that screw caps on wine make it look cheap. Jennifer is so disillusioned with the company's new direction, she can easily see why her fellow coworkers are disengaged.

8.2.1 Challenge 1: The Researcher Bias Challenge

In our story, Jennifer has fallen victim to a very common challenge we all face. It is human nature to have opinions, and with technology resources as they are today, it is easy to find support for those opinions that can feel like data if you go into a situation without eyes wide open. Bias is also affected by support or opposition of senior leaders at a company. When your bias is in line with the opinion of leadership, it can feel like a 100% proven fact. When your bias is not in line with senior leaders, as in our story, it can lead you to search out others who agree with you and alienate your opinions from the truth. Both polarize our opinions, forcing them to the black or white side of the spectrum, when often the truth truly is gray.

To combat the researcher bias challenge, it is important for consultants to reserve judgment until far after the planning stage of any engagement. Having opinions is one thing, allowing those opinions to influence your data collection and preparation can be dangerous. Instead, focus on the facts and share only the facts, not a string of opinions, as you move through planning for any organizational diagnosis and assessment engagement.

8.2.2 Challenge 2: The Fear of Change Challenge

As discussed in the chapter introduction, fear of change is a real human emotion. In the story above, was it fear of change enticing Jennifer and others to rebel against the new company direction? Possibly, but if asked, Jennifer and her coworkers might not vocalize the feelings they have as fear. They just know that they are not happy with the company direction and feel that things were better in the old days.

Longing for and embellishment of the "good old days" is a clear indicator of the Fear of Change Challenge. It is dangerous, because it often keeps companies from moving forward in a world constantly progressing. As has been quoted often by many leaders, if we are not moving forward, we are falling behind. In business today, standing still is no longer an option, and therefore fear of change can and should be addressed. And the best way to address this challenge is through sold communication and engagement. As part of the planning stage, design a communications plan you will use to communicate the initiative process with stakeholders. And remember, stakeholders are not only sitting in the C-suite of companies. Build a plan that will allow you to communicate early, communicate often, and communicate thoroughly through the company. A solid communications plans should also include communication check points to ensure the right message is getting to all levels of the company.

Remember, absent information, human nature is to fill in the blanks. My experience has shown that what people fill into those blanks, the story they create, is often far more sinister than the true story, so take steps in the planning of any initiative to stop this from happening. You should also plan to build a contingency plan to search out and combat rumors and misinformation when they appear.

8.2.3 Challenge 3: The Planning Do-Loop Challenge

Another challenge that can often come up in the planning step is the Do-Loop Challenge. Do-Loop is a computer programming term that refers to a statement built into computer code that enables a computer to repeat a set of steps forever (or until some stated condition is reached). In the planning step of an organizational diagnosis, this refers to the tendency to continually plan and plan, while never making any step toward the next steps in the process (collecting data).

This can result from many things, including the two challenges mentioned above. Fear of change and researcher bias can keep an initiative in the planning stage forever. Other contributors to a planning Do-Loop can include, over the top benchmarking, the imagined need for 100% consensus, or the theory you need to wait for the perfect time to make something happen.

A word of advice, timing will never be perfect, everyone will never 100% agree on anything, and competitors will change and grow, so you will never know everything about everyone. Instead, take enough time in the planning stage and then dive into the next step. A strong planning phase should end with a plan that is actionable, but flexible enough to allow for adjustment and change when real life hinders perfect planning. As long as you remember this, you will avoid the Planning Do-Loop.

8.2.4 Challenge 4: The Mission Creep Challenge

I would be remiss if I did not include just a few sentences to address Mission Creep in this section. Mission Creep is a phrase we use to refer to an engagement in which the mission (or goal) of the engagement is not clearly defined or keeps adjusting a little bit at a time over the duration of the project. In these cases, the engagement turns into the Energizer Bunny, it keeps going and going, with no end and no success in sight. This is especially dangerous when fixed fee contracts are written and consultants cannot be paid for additional work.

To avoid Mission Creep, build a strong project scope during the planning phase of any engagement. Define the project deliverables in clear, measurable language. An unclear goal would be something like "Improve employee engagement" while a clear goal would be "Increase participation in after work engagement events by 50%." Do you see the difference? You could spend the next 5000 years improving employee engagement, but it is easy to know when you have reached a point where 10 more employees come to a company-sponsored engagement event. And finally, always leave room for engaging in a new contract. Know that you cannot and will not be able to address all organizational opportunities in one sitting. Do not be afraid to engage in discussions about new opportunities that appear as you move through an initiative. The key is making sure you contract for those new opportunities. Formalize new opportunities into a new contracted engagement and avoid creep.

8.3 Challenges That Can Arise in Collecting and Analyzing Data

Ben has been running his OD consulting business for nearly 10 years. He is an expert in change management. A new client, a major player in the oil and gas industry, has contacted him, asking for help in revamping their current safety program.

During initial meetings, Ben is impressed by the commitment of the team to this issue. He learns quickly that a task force has been put together by the CEO herself, tasked with making a step change in safety for the company. The task force comprises top managers from all over the company, and Ben is excited to have been called in by the leader of the task force as a process advisor. As Ben walks into the first meeting, he is introduced to the team as "the answer to our prayers" by the task force leader. "Here's the guy that is going to give us all of the answers we need!"

Ben states that he is excited to begin work with the group to determine why the company's once stellar safety record is faltering. He lays out a detailed data collection plan, which involves talking to individuals at all levels of the company and benchmarking other companies in the oil and gas industry and alternate industries where safety is a major concern.

His plan is met with pushback from the task force. Two concerns immediately came to the surface. The task force does not want Ben speaking to the CEO or anyone in the C-suite because they have been assigned with fixing this problem and the senior leaders should not be bothered. The members of the task force can share the thoughts and speak for the C-suite. Benchmarking studies have already been performed within the industry and members of the task force see no point in diluting the data by adding in studies from industries outside of the oil and gas space. Besides, they are in a hurry and need answers quickly, and we all know benchmarking takes time.

8.3.1 Challenge 1: The Expert Challenge

Ben's first red flag should have gone up the second he walked into the room and was introduced as the "guy that will give us the answer." While, as OD consultants, we should have a reputation as thought leaders in our fields, we should never be the only voice in the room. Clients looking for the easy answer and quick fix from a consultant are not looking for an OD engagement. As we all know, for a true OD experience to happen, the client must be committed to discovery and deployment.

In the above story, a faltering safety record will not be fixed by a quick training program. Often, the presenting problem (an increase in safety violations) is simply a symptom of numerous problems that must be explored and addressed through the initiative. This should be clarified to the client early in the process to avoid this situation.

8.3.2 Challenge 2: The Challenge of Limited Range

A second alarm should have went off in Ben's head when he described his data collection plan and was told that he would not have access to the C-suite during data collection. This happens more than we would like to admit. That does not mean that people on the task force are trying to hide information. As they see it, they are simply doing their jobs as assigned by the CEO. But in an initiative like the one described here, direct access to the C-suite is critical. C-suite support is critical to achieve the support and stakeholder buy-in needed to successfully complete an initiative of this sort, but also because there will need to be messaging coming from the C-suite to show support for something as organizationally important as this OD initiative.

Again, the key to avoiding this challenge is to be sure you engage both the economic buyer and the strategic buyer in the proposal and contacting phase of an initiative. Scope the project correctly and detail the resources you will need to succeed. Ensure that you include all individuals with whom you wish to speak in the project scope. If you don't know their names, include departments or titles. This will ensure you are able to speak with everyone you should in order to gather the data that you need.

8.3.3 Challenge 3: The Challenge of Limited Time

There is never enough time, ever. And when you have a client tell you there is not enough time to complete a full data collection cycle for a major OD project, it should cause pause. Much like in the planning phase, while you do not want to get caught in a data-collection Do-Loop, you need to ensure that you scope the project to allow for enough time to collect the optimal amount of data needed to make recommendations.

This does not mean you pad your deliverable timeline to include a huge fudge-factor. Instead, the key is to fully detail a deliverable schedule based on the project objectives. Outlining milestone check points can also help to ensure that you do not get hung up with this challenge.

8.3.4 Challenge 4: The Challenge of Been-There-Done-That

If you are being called into a company to complete an organizational assessment and diagnosis, odds are that someone within the company has also been tasked with looking into the issue at some point in time. It is essential to connect with any individuals within the company in this position and to review the documents they have produced to avoid reinventing the wheel. These individuals can also be sources of deep company data and strong allies. But what should be avoided, to avoid the Been-There-Done-That Challenge, is the tendency to assume that once something is done, it is done forever.

In our story, the task force decided that since they already completed an industry-wide benchmarking survey, no additional benchmarking was needed. I would strongly advise against taking a statement like that at face value. In the data-collection phase, it may be necessary to revisit and redo the past data collections. Previously collected data should be evaluated on a case-by-case basis and with great care. Using your outside eyes, sort through what has been collected looking for holes, work with the team to verify whether those holes truly exist, and collaboratively build a plan to close those data gaps.

8.3.5 Challenge 5: The Challenge of Not-Going-There-Not-Doing-That

Another challenge in the same family as the one we have just explored is the Not-Going-There-Not-Doing-That Challenge. In our story, when Ben suggested that they also benchmark companies outside of their current industry, the task force pushed back hard. You will recall the feeling was that any new data from outside the industry would be irrelevant and dilute the data they have already collected.

I hope you all appreciate the value of looking outside of one's own industry for innovation. Often, when engaging in a consulting relationship with a new client, the conversation starts with a statement from the client about how unique their market and challenges are. After over 15 years in the business, I can truly and loudly say that is simply not true. Humans are humans. Yes, markets are slightly different, cultures are slightly different, and organizations are slightly different, but we often have more in common than we have at odds. Much is learned from the world, and if we limit our investigation to only a small subset of business and industry, we will miss things.

8.4 Challenges That Can Arise in Feeding Back Data

After a recent company restructuring, Laura has been chosen to lead an internal team to complete a corporate climate survey of her organization. She is excited to be involved in such a highly visible project that will set the tone for the organization. She leads her team through an exhaustive data-collection process, interviewing members of each unit in the organization. The team also creates and distributes a survey to the entire organization. The 80% response rate they receive is amazing, and they are thrilled to have so much data to report back to the CEO.

In analyzing the data, it becomes apparent that employees at the company are not as happy as they could be. There is a strong sense that senior leadership is disengaged and out of touch with the everyday worker. Quotes such as "The recent restricting did little to impact the overall success of my unit" and "The recent restructuring here made me very afraid because my supervisor keep me in the dark and didn't share what was going through the minds of senior leaders" are common themes pulled from the interviews. In addition, over three-quarters of the survey respondents state that policies are inconsistent across units and feel like supervisors are not following the stated company procedures.

Even with these negative findings, Laura is happy to see that employees seem to feel very favorable about the working relationships they have with others in their teams. Over and over again, interviewees said that the working relationships that they have with their colleagues is the best part of their day.

In preparing the data to be shared with the senior leadership team, Laura focuses on the good and mentions the negative feedback quickly at the end in a "Suggestions for Moving Forward" section of the report. Without getting into too much detail, she suggests that a supervisor training program would help the organization. The suggestions are met with pushback from the CEO, who states that is it obvious that since the surveys and interviews were completed shortly after a major restricting, people were just angry. She is sure that if the survey was done again in a few months, the results would be much more favorable.

8.4.1 Challenge 1: The I-Don't-Believe-You Challenge

In the above story, Laura fell victim to this challenge for the fear of overstating employee dissatisfaction. Because she focused on the good and only mentioned the findings about supervisor shortcoming as a suggestion, much of the data to support this finding was lost.

Laura's predicament is not a new one. No one likes giving negative feedback because we all know that when people face hearing negative or constructive feedback, their initial reaction is often to get defensive. Instead of avoiding giving negative feedback, build a plan to deliver the feedback in a way to avoid the bad reaction. Do this by ensuring that the message you deliver is backed up by verifiable evidence and examples. In the story above, instead of saying "supervisors would benefit from training," it would have been much more impactful for Laura to present direct quotes from the interviews that represented the opinions of the employees interviewed. Limit feedback to short, digestible segments, and check in often with the receiver to ensure they remain engaged and open.

Since trust also plays an important part in feedback, it is essential to come to the feedback part of any situation from a place of honesty. Separate information from emotion, and honestly feedback data, not opinions. In this way, you can make a case for change and avoid the defensiveness that bubbles up sometimes in these conversations.

8.4.2 Challenge 2: The Scapegoat Challenge

Sometimes the challenge is not that the feedback receiver does not believe you, but instead that they want to blame the findings on a scapegoat. Scapegoating, in this context, means placing the blame for a negative finding on a prior corporate initiative and assuming that the negativity will eventually dissipate all by itself.

In the story above, the CEO has decided that it is the recent restructuring that is causing the surprising low employee satisfaction, not anything more. Once this decision has been made, it would be easy for the CEO to discredit all learnings from the interviews and survey, and blame the dissatisfaction on that factor. The statement that things will automatically get better in a few months shows the CEO's disinterest in hearing any data to the contrary.

To combat scapegoating, provide full data as part of your feedback session. If you can do that through the voices of those interviewed using direct, anonymous, quotes, all the better. Laura did a great job collecting data from across the organization and should have been able to build a strong, consistent message to deliver to the CEO. Just like in the first challenge, delivering this data as fact, without emotion, would help to eliminate the scapegoating defense. It is also critical to note that even in times of turbulence, like a restructuring, situations rarely get better all by themselves.

8.4.3 Challenge 3: The Limited Acceptance Challenge

Another challenge we often see when feeding back data relates to how fully the feedback is accepted, and how fully leaders wish to engage in discussions related to determining their next steps (or solution set) around those findings. In our story, because the CEO did not fully accept the feedback regarding the need for a supervisor training program, she dismisses the idea and any guidance related to that finding. Let's say the training program was one of the five findings that came up during this OD assessment. Odds are, even if a plan is developed, embraced, and implemented to address the other four findings, ignoring one will have consequences. Progress will stall, leadership will get frustrated, the good work will be thrown out, and the entire OD engagement will end in failure. All of this simply because one finding was ignored.

In the real world, this happens a lot, for reasons like those stated here (disbelief or scapegoating) or for much nobler reasons such as asset availability and time. Often, when given a list of findings, organizations will work to solve the easiest and implement the cheapest fix, and may avoid discussions around those findings that cost the most time and money, or elicit the most headache and heartburn. This puts the entire initiative at risk, especially when an action plan has been built assuming all findings will be addressed.

To combat the Limited Acceptance Challenge, it is important for practitioners to identify the impact of ignoring findings. We must first determine how skipping over a finding or hiding/ignoring the data connected to it will affect the overall OD initiative. By fully describing those potentials and ensuring consequences for skipping over findings are fully understood, you can ensure that the strategic impact on the overall OD initiative is clear.

8.5 Challenges That Can Arise during Action Planning

Action planning is Christos's favorite part of any OD assessment and diagnosis process. As a natural project manager, he looks at the action planning step as a key to success, a systematic process needed to succeed in any change effort. Christos knows this can only be accomplished by using sound change models and principles, so he is surprised when the team that he has been working with for the last year on a major change effort wants to skim though the action planning process.

When he tries to implement a model he has used in similar change efforts over the years, he gets pushback. The team feels that they are clear on the issues discovered during the data-collection phase of the project, and the feedback part went so well, they assume that everyone is on the same page. There is no need to outline what they all know they need to do.

Because of his concerns, Christos goes to the CEO to discuss his fear. He is surprised to learn that the CEO is equally complacent to this final step. While the CEO was excited at the start of the project, it appears he has been kept out of conversations and is now not only unclear on the team's progress, but also unclear on the need for change.

Christos feels stuck and does not know what to do next. He goes back to the team to discuss his conversation with the CEO, which just further derails the team's conversations around action planning.

The team begins the change process anyway, without a clear action plan. They get three months into the change initiative and someone from outside the team asks how it is going. They try to answer, but with no clear milestones to measure, all they can say is "it seems to be going fine." When questioned further about what this means, no one on the team can detail what has happened. Yet, they keep moving. But as they do, their excitement fades. People on the team seem to lose interest and things start getting missed. The effort derails. People give up. And the CEO says "I knew it wouldn't work, let's try something else right away. I'll form a new task force and get something going next week."

8.5.1 Challenge 1: The We've Got This Challenge

The team with which Christos is working in the above story has fallen victim to the We've Got This Challenge. This happens easily, when working with a very involved team passionate about a project. They have lived and breathed the details of this initiative for a year, so it can be expected that they think everyone else in the organization is equally aware, on board, and ready to move on making change. Rarely, if ever, is this the case. And even if, by some miracle, everyone in the organization is as engaged as the change team, action planning is needed to make sure that everyone is stepping in time through the entire change effort, from start to finish.

Planning may seem like overkill when the leaders in a change effort knows exactly what they want to do, but even then, it is critical to keep the project moving forward. Without an action plan, steps will get skipped, missed, enacted out of order, or just screwed up. Take the time to build an actionable plan to keep this from happening, even if you feel that everyone on the team is working in tandem and on the same page.

8.5.2 Challenge 2: The We Don't Know How Far We've Come Challenge

In our story, when asked about progress, the team cannot provide much of an answer. Without an action plan that details the path and milestones along that path, how can anyone on the team discuss progress in anything above anecdotal terms? They cannot.

Instead, by developing a plan for monitoring and managing the progress of a project, anyone could measure progress to milestones, report outcomes, deliver feedback, and record successes. This allows team members and others the opportunity to tell the story of change, a critical step in keeping the initiative moving forward and the organization engaged.

8.5.3 Challenge 3: The We're Lost Challenge

As we have said, change is a difficult process, so a detailed plan is necessary to keep people on track and moving in the right direction. In our story, we see what happens when the project falls apart. Dred, feelings of failure, people jumping ship...and you are lost.

Using a strong action plan will keep this from happening. A strong plan should include clearly stated activities that are actionably linked to goals.

Avoid broadly generalized steps, which can allow people to unintentionally get lost. For most complex efforts, it is necessary to link the discrete, actionable activities in a time sequenced plan, showing individuals how they need to maneuver from point A to point B to point C. Through these steps, you act like a GPS, keeping the team on task, excited, and moving forward in the right direction.

8.5.4 Challenge 4: The We've Gone This Far and Now We're Sunk Challenge

So again, in the story, we see what can happen after people get lost. The effort is ended, forgotten, or ignored in relation to the next project. Even if the project does not go as phenomenally wrong as it does in our story, bumps will happen. The best way to rebound from the We've Gone This Far and Now We're Sunk Challenge is contingency planning.

Contingency planning is the key to ensuring that plans are not derailed when bumps come up. In building a strong contingency plan in an OD assessment and diagnosis effort, it is critical to think about potential interruptions and how the organization will address them. In this part of the planning process, it is important to list any foreseeable interruptions to the plan and ideas on how they can be overcome if they happen. This step is often skipped because of the fear that by thinking about contingency plans, the group will not be fully committed to change. But, if it is presented in a positive light, this will not happen. Instead of saying, "This is the contingency plan we'll use if our initial plan fails," think more like "We're going through a contingency planning process so that we'll be agile if and when disruptions happen." By reframing the thinking, a contingency plan moves from a fix to a preparation.

8.5.5 Challenge 5: The We're Not Committed Challenge

In our story, we can see early that the CEO is not committed. In his meeting with Christos, he is already showing his disengagement. It is not surprising that at the end of the story, once the initiative falls apart, he abandons the effort and starts something new.

In this example, the CEO's lack of commitment seems to stem from not being kept in the loop as the team progressed through their process. As we have said before, communication is a critical step in all organizational diagnosis and assessment efforts. Avoiding the We're Not Committed

Challenge is just one more reason to have a strong communications plan as a part of your action plan.

But like anything, loss of commitment can come from many triggers. When people do not feel like their opinions have been heard in the assessment process, commitment fades. When people get distracted by the newest, shiniest thing on the scene, commitment can falter. When people feel lost, commitment definitely can come to an end. To avoid this challenge, it is critical to follow the steps outlined in earlier chapters that ensure a strong organizational diagnosis and assessment effort.

8.5.6 Challenge 6: The We're Moving, but the Organization Isn't Challenge

So, what happens if part of the organization is committed, but others are not? Easy; company cultural change will not happen and you face the We're Moving, but the Organization Isn't Challenge. In our story, the initiative falls apart from not having a strong action plan and not having a committed champion and senior leadership team. But even if the team had the best action plan in the world, without commitment from the senior team, the initiative might have been in trouble.

In our story, the team should have worked to avoid this challenge by engaging with the CEO on a regularly agreed upon schedule to ensure that he remained committed, both culturally and financially. For others in the company, this challenge can be avoided by recording progress and sharing successes, so you can tell the corporate story of change. You need to have team members, senior leaders, and corporate influencers echoing the story through their actions and communications. By taking these steps, initiatives will become part of the organizational culture, and that is the only way to ensure a successful effort.

8.6 Chapter Summary

In this chapter, we have explored what can go wrong in the four major steps of organizational diagnosis and assessment. We have discussed that as with any initiative, bumps will happen along the way. The key to keeping a small detour from turning into a major detailer is being prepared. By spending time at the onset of each step building and communicating a strong plan, you can avoid many challenges that may arise. It is also critical to remain flexible as these processes ensue. The days of moving quickly and easily from point A to point B are gone. Today, as we travel to point B, it is moving, so our plans must be nimble enough to track the changes in our destination caused by the normal movement of the business market and smart enough to adjust to meet B where it ends up.

Remember, people often think of success as a straight line up; always rising, always up, and up at a right angle. We know projects can often start off in a strong, upward momentum, but can then quickly turn into a jumbled ball of twists and turns in the middle. By having a strong, well-developed plan, you can navigate through those twists and turns to come out of the other side at that same strong, upward angle to success.

8.7 The OD Assessment and Diagnosis Challenges Quick Reference Tool

Planning for Assessment and Feedback Challenges

The Researcher Bias Challenge
Key: Remain Natural
<ul><li>Reserve judgment</li><li>Do not let opinions influence data collection and preparation</li><li>Focus on the facts of the situation</li><li>Share only the facts, not a string of opinions</li></ul>
The Fear of Change Challenge
Key: Combat Fear with Information
<ul><li>Admit that change is scary</li><li>Know that sometimes fear of change materializes in ways that are difficult to articulate</li><li>Articulate that through change, we can survive and thrive</li><li>Build and follow a solid communication and engagement plan</li><li>Check communication and engagement progress often</li><li>Search out and combat rumors and misinformation immediately</li></ul>
The Planning Do-Loop Challenge
Key: Plan and Move, Don't Just Plan
<ul><li>Realize this challenge can be a symptom of other challenges</li><li>Accept that timing will never be perfect, 100% conscious is not mandatory, and markets continually change</li><li>End your planning phase with an actionable, flexible plan</li></ul>

(*Continued*)

The Mission Creep Challenge
Key: Scope, Deliver, Evaluate, and Reengage
• Scope all projects realistically • Define deliverables in clear, measurable language • Seek opportunities for follow-up contracts

Collecting and Analyzing Data Challenges

The Expert Challenge
Key: Engage, Don't Advise
• Set reasonable client expectations regarding what they must contribute • Ensure you are not seen as or act as the only voice in the room • Engage clients in discovery and deployment
The Challenge of Limited Range
Key: Engage Everyone
• Set reasonable client expectations regarding needed resources • Engage both the economic and the strategic buyers • Scope the project correctly • Detail a person- or position-engagement plan as part of the project scope
The Challenge of Limited Time
Key: Scope Appropriately
• Set reasonable client expectations regarding time • Fully detail a deliverable schedule based on the project objectives • Outline milestone check points
The Challenge of Been-There-Done-That
Key: Identify Data Gaps
• Connect with individuals who have already worked on the initiative • Review existing research, documents, policies, and procedures • Use your outside eyes to look for holes (data gaps) • Work with the team to verify the validity of data gaps • Collaboratively build a plan to close data gaps
The Challenge of Not-Going-There-Not-Doing-That
Key: Look Around
• Do not be afraid to look outside the industry for innovation • Realize and share that there is much to learn from the world • Do not limit investigation to a small subset of business and industry

(Continued)

Feeding Back Data Challenges

The I-Don't-Believe-You Challenge
Key: Avoid Avoidance
<ul><li>Do not avoid giving negative or constructive feedback, instead, deliver it with a plan</li><li>Ensure that the message you deliver is backed up by verifiable evidence and examples</li><li>Limit feedback to short, digestible segments</li><li>Check in often with the receiver to ensure they remain engaged and open</li><li>Know the importance of trust</li><li>Come to any feedback situation from a place of honesty</li><li>Separate information from emotion</li><li>Feedback data, not opinions</li></ul>
The Scapegoat Challenge
Key: Avoid Blame
<ul><li>Provide full data as part of your feedback session</li><li>Use other voices besides your own</li><li>Deliver data as fact, without emotion</li><li>Know that even in turbulent times, things do not just get better all by themselves</li><li>Challenge others who blame findings on a person or past situation or who over-generalize findings</li></ul>
The Limited Acceptance Challenge
Key: Share the Consequences
<ul><li>Map how the findings link directly to data gathered</li><li>Show how findings build and interact</li><li>Discuss consequences of ignoring or hiding data related to all findings</li><li>Present findings as an integrated package, not a pick-and-choose menu</li></ul>

Action Planning Challenges

The We've Got This Challenge
Key: Build the Map
<ul><li>Do not allow the importance of action planning to be minimized</li><li>Remind team members that not everyone is as aware of the project as they are</li><li>Remind team members that not everyone is as committed to the project as they are</li><li>Build a plan of detailed, actionable steps</li><li>Avoid skipping, missing, and enacting steps out of order</li></ul>

(Continued)

The We Don't Know How Far We've Come Challenge
Key: Discuss Progress
• Develop a plan for monitoring and managing the process of a project • Measure progress to milestones • Report outcomes • Deliver feedback to the entire organization • Record and share successes
The We're Lost Challenge
Key: Follow Your Map
• Use your plan to keep people on track and moving forward • Build your plan with clearly stated activities that are actionably linked to goals • Avoid broadly generalized steps • Link the discrete, actionable activities in a time-sequenced plan
The We've Gone This Far and Now We're Sunk Challenge
Key: Contingency Planning
• Think about potential interruptions • Decide how the organization will address potential interruptions • Present the plan in a positive light • Have a contingency plan in place to avoid derailment
The We're Not Committed Challenge
Key: Re-engagement
• Build a communications plan to keep all stakeholders engaged • Know the triggers for noncommitment and avoid them • Ensure everyone feels that they have been heard • Plan for distractions and re-engagement • When people feel lost, find them
The We're Moving, but the Organization Isn't Challenge
Key: Build a New Culture
• Ensure you have a strong action plan and project champion • Ensure you have a link to the senior leadership team • Engage with project champions and stakeholders on a regularly agreed upon schedule • Record progress and share successes organization-wide • Work to have team members, senior leaders, and corporate influencers echoing the stories of success

8.8 Keys to Remember: A Model for Assessing Organizations and Planning Action

In this book, we have presented a model for Assessing Organizations and Planning Action based on the research of the authors and editors. Building off of the self-assessment worksheet at the end of Chapter 2, and as a final checklist for moving forward, we would like to offer practitioners the below tool originally created by Dr. William J. Rothwell for ensuring you have considered everything necessary when undertaking assessment and diagnosis in your own organization and/or in your client' organizations.

Organization Assessment—Planning	
	Involve the right people in the project
	Clarify the desired goals and outcomes of the assessment
	Agree on what and who will be assessed
	Choose methods
	Determine how to best collect data
	Determine how to analyze and report the data
	Determine how to feedback and utilize the data
	Agree with leaders on the process and how the results will be utilized
	Coach leaders on their role in making the assessment successful
	Develop milestones for getting things done
Organization Assessment—Data Collection	
	Assure that anyone involved in performing the assessment is properly trained
	Prepare the organization for the assessment
	Perform the assessment
Organization Assessment—Data Analysis	
	Develop a strategy for analyzing and presenting the assessment results in a user-friendly way
	Prepare a simple way to understand and use presentation findings

(Continued)

Organization Assessment—Data Feedback	
	Design a feedback strategy for determining who gets what information how and when
	Prepare the appropriate people on how to use the results for helpful and not harmful purposes
	Decide on when and how to connect the feedback to action-planning
	Prepare people for how to understand and utilize the data in helpful and positive ways
	Diffuse anxiety and assure that the process will be a beneficial and useful one
Organization Action Planning—Involve Key Stakeholders	
	Involve those who are in the best position to understand and utilize the assessment and lead needed changes
	Insure that someone will lead the change effort and, if needed, develop a change team to plan and manage the change process
Organization Action Planning—Evaluate and Prioritize Relevant Data	
	Develop a process for evaluating, prioritizing, and making the assessment information manageable and useable
	Clarify the focus of the change efforts (whole organization, group or intergroup, individual, structural, technological, etc.)
	Consider the level of desired change (fine tuning, incremental, or transformational)
	Focus on present realities, future ideals, and possibilities
	Explore alternatives for achieving greater success
Organization Action Planning—Agree on the Changes to Be Made	
	Agree on the actions to be taken recognizing that it is better to do a few things well than many things poorly
	Evaluate the change from a systems' perspective considering the implications of the changes and the alignment needed
Organization Action Planning—Develop a Change Strategy	
	Identify any forces working for or against the desired change
	Explore strategy alternatives

(*Continued*)

	Develop a change process based on a sound change model
	Develop a process for monitoring and managing the change process
Organization Action Planning—Clarify Roles and Follow-Through Responsibilities	
	Clarify the roles and follow-through responsibilities of all involved in the change process
	Commit to keeping the change process as clear and simple as possible to improve both the health and effectiveness of the organization

Bibliography

Bruce, R., and Wyman, S. 1998. *Changing Organizations, Practicing Action Training and Research*. Thousand Oaks, CA: Sage Publications, Inc.

Duhigg, C. 2014. *The Power of Habit: What We Do What We Do in Life and Business*. New York: Random House Trade Paperbacks.

Dyckman, J. M., and Cutler, J. A. 2003. *Scapegoats at Work: Taking the Bull's-Eye Off Your Back*. Westport, CT: Praeger.

Rothwell, W. J., Stavros, J. M., Sullivan, R. L., and Sullivan, A. (eds.). 2010. *Practicing Organization Development: A Guide for Leading Change* (3rd ed.). San Francisco, CA: Pfeiffer.

Seese, M. 2010. *Scrappy Business Contingency Planning: How to Bullet-Proof Your Business and Laugh at Volcanoes, Tornadoes, Locust Plagues, and Hard Drive Crashes*. Cupertino, CA: Scrappy About.

Additional Online Resources

Numerous resources related to project management, avoiding scapegoating and mission creep, and others: http://www.projectmanagement.com/ (accessed October 4, 2016).

Numerous resources related to project management, time management, contingency planning, and others: https://www.mindtools.com/ (accessed October 4, 2016).

Risk Impact/Probability Chart worksheet tool is available here: https://www.mind-tools.com/pages/article/newPPM_78.htm (accessed October 4, 2016).

What If Analysis tools: https://www.mindtools.com/pages/article/newTED_76.htm (accessed October 4, 2016).

Chapter 9

Conclusion and Future Directions of Diagnosis and Assessment for Organization Development

William J. Rothwell

Contents

What is the future of organizational assessment and diagnosis in organization development (OD)? This chapter addresses this simple yet profound question by offering 10 predictions for the future of organizational assessment and diagnosis:

- Prediction 1: OD will face increasing challenges as people grow weary from too many and too frequent assessment efforts.
- Prediction 2: Assessment and diagnosis will be conducted faster using mobile technology.
- Prediction 3: Assessment and diagnosis methods will turn as much to spurring innovation as to identifying problems or leveraging strengths.
- Prediction 4: The importance of trust will grow more apparent in conducting useful organizational assessment and diagnosis.
- Prediction 5: Group decision support systems and collaboration software will make it easier to encourage organizational assessment and diagnosis.
- Prediction 6: Big data will make it easier to collect data about organizational assessment and diagnosis from secondary sources.
- Prediction 7: Internal and external OD practitioners will become more sophisticated in their approaches to conducting organizational assessment and diagnosis.
- Prediction 8: Organizational stakeholders will become more assertive about having a say in organizational assessment and diagnosis.

- Prediction 9: Empirical research will reveal the most important issues to examine when conducting organizational assessment and diagnosis.
- Prediction 10: More efforts will be made to integrate descriptive and prescriptive approaches to organizational assessment and diagnosis.

9.1 Prediction 1: OD Will Face Increasing Challenges as People Grow Weary from Too Many and Too Frequent Assessment Efforts

When people are asked to make too many changes in too little time, they fight (resist) change, flee from change, or become paralyzed and inactive. With software such as Survey Monkey that makes it easier to create and send surveys and increasing efforts by organizations to collect data on many issues from their workforces, workers are experiencing too many efforts to capture their perceptions. They respond by resisting data collection, trying to avoid those efforts, or simply ignoring them. That is especially true if efforts have been made to collect data from them and nothing was done or communicated based on the information the individual provided.

Look for this problem to grow worse. Software and other automated systems (such as automatic dialing and voice input-output technology) make it too easy to collect data. But people are growing weary of the collection of so much data. And they will continue to disengage as they are unsure who will get the data, what they will do with it, and how it may affect the respondent.

9.2 Prediction 2: Assessment and Diagnosis Will Be Conducted Faster Using Mobile Technology

Mobile devices such as smartphones, tablets, and wearable technology such as watches and glasses provide vehicles for collecting data as part of organizational assessment and diagnosis. It is possible to record and measure almost every human experience through mobile technology and increasingly smart software applications. Customers may be polled for their reactions to organizational experiences immediately after they have lived through them; employees can be polled for their thoughts even while in a business meeting or conference. It is becoming easier and more cost-effective to collect 360-degree data on almost anything, and that data can be used in organizational assessment and diagnosis. Soon, everything people do will be recorded and measured. The problem in the future will not be collecting data; rather, it will focus on identifying the most important data that is worth collecting and using.

9.3 Prediction 3: Assessment and Diagnosis Methods Will Turn as Much to Spurring Innovation as to Identifying Problems or Leveraging Strengths

Many business observers claim that the world's economy is shifting from information-based to innovation-based. OD practitioners of the future will be tasked to help organizations establish and sustain creative work cultures that encourage worker innovation to outsmart competitors by finding new, cost-effective ways to source supplies, produce goods or deliver services, discover and develop talent, increase customer satisfaction and grow market share, and build customer loyalty. Organizational leaders are likely to move beyond traditional problem-solving-based approaches and strength-finding approaches to finding new, creative ways to regard the issues and act on that innovation.

OD practitioners must become more familiar with data gathering approaches that spur innovation. Some overlap with well-known methods to solve problems. Others are drawn from fields such as advertising and marketing, where creative approaches have long been prized. These approaches should be applied to organizational assessment and diagnosis.

9.4 Prediction 4: The Importance of Trust Will Grow More Apparent in Conducting Useful Organizational Assessment and Diagnosis

OD practitioners have long focused on trust issues in organizational settings. Organizational leaders sometimes call in external consultants because consultants are more objective, and less prone to internal political influences, than insiders. Without trust, people will not share what they really think with anyone. In low trust work settings, workers will feel psychologically uncomfortable and will engage in risk averse behavior negatively correlated to productivity and to innovation. Turnover will be high, absenteeism will be high, and workers will not openly discuss problems with each other, or with their immediate supervisors out of fear of repercussions—such as becoming the next statistic on a downsizing list.

More work should be done on measuring trust levels at the outset of organizational assessment and to discovering ways to increase trust levels when they are so low as to pose obstacles to meaningful organizational assessment.

9.5 Prediction 5: Group Decision Support Systems and Collaboration Software Will Make It Easier to Encourage Organizational Assessment and Diagnosis

Group decision support systems (GDSS) automate identifying issues, gathering data about those issues, feeding back the data in real time to stakeholders, and facilitating decision-making aimed to pinpoint problems, prioritize them, discover solutions to the problems, plan actions to implement the solutions, and measure effective change. *Collaboration software* permits users to work on the same documents or spreadsheets at the same time, thereby encouraging stakeholders to provide inputs to decision-making and increase their involvement levels in the decision process.

Both GDSS and collaboration software may have roles to play in organizational assessment. They have been used for that purpose, though the literature to support that assertion is sparse. Look for GDSS and collaboration software to be used more frequently because they encourage data collection in real time across geographical settings quickly when used properly.

9.6 Prediction 6: Big Data Will Make It Easier to Collect Data about Organizational Assessment and Diagnosis from Secondary Sources

As a counterbalance to the trend of software and hardware that makes it easier to collect data for organizational assessment from individuals through surveys and other methods, big data makes it easier to diminish active data collection from people and rely on secondary data gathered during normal business operations. Look for more OD clients to ask how big data might be substituted for active data collection to reduce the time and effort needed by individuals to provide information. OD practitioners must be prepared to become more selective on what data to collect, from whom to collect it, how it is collected, why it is collected, and what is to be done with it.

9.7 Prediction 7: Internal and External OD Practitioners Will Become More Sophisticated in Their Approaches to Conducting Organizational Assessment and Diagnosis

Some consulting firms have already made their organizational assessment approaches an issue related to their branding. For instance, McKinsey is well known for its 7-S Model, and that model provides a strategic branding issue for that consulting firm. Clients know what model will be used to conduct the organizational assessment. This type of consistent approach has the advantage of being easily explained to clients, reducing any anxiety about what data will be collected during an organizational assessment.

Considering the quality and quantity of publications available on organizational assessment, more OD practitioners will probably grow increasingly sophisticated in their approaches to organizational assessment. Evidence already exists that some consulting firms, advertising on the web, tout a consistent approach to examining organizations. Those firms use their organizational assessment approach as a way to define their brand and provide their firms with competitive advantage.

9.8 Prediction 8: Organizational Stakeholders Will Become More Assertive about Having a Say in Organizational Assessment and Diagnosis

In many organizations today, managers insist on having a major say in organizational assessment. They sometimes limit consultant access to certain groups; they try to influence how (or whether) organizational assessment is conducted; they influence how data are collected; they influence how data are fed back to those who provided it; and they can use organizational assessment information in ways that are sometimes outside the control of OD practitioners.

But, in the future, look for more organizational stakeholders, beyond managers, to grow more assertive about having a say in organizational assessment and diagnosis. Customers, stockholders, government regulators, and employee groups (such as protected class employees) may insist on participating in shaping the plan for organizational assessment, administering data collection, analyzing results, and feeding back data to various groups. This growing assertiveness stems from consumer activism, a desire by all stakeholder groups to have more say in issues affecting them, and a fundamental distrust of organizational managers.

9.9 Prediction 9: Empirical Research Will Reveal the Most Important Issues to Examine When Conducting Organizational Assessment and Diagnosis

A big challenge facing any OD practitioner when conducting an organizational assessment is exactly what to look at. Organizations are complex. It is difficult to narrow down issues in a comprehensive organizational assessment or to focus issues to examine in a situational organizational assessment. Recall that a *comprehensive organizational assessment* is a broad-brush look at an entire organization or a part, whereas a *situational organizational assessment* is centered on a specific problem or issue of concern to one or more stakeholders.

But the base of research literature is growing on what matters most on many organizational issues. As a simple example, much research has been conducted on the High Performance Workplace, defined as a workplace that encourage high productivity, much research has been conducted on the competencies required of managers to inspire innovation among their workers, research has been conducted on human resource strategies with the most impact on organizational profitability, and much more. A substantial research literature exists on what matters about organizational performance, safety, profitability, worker engagement, and other issues of importance to leaders. The challenge is for OD practitioners to put this literature together in an integrated framework. Look for that to happen.

9.10 Prediction 10: More Efforts Will Be Made to Integrate Descriptive and Prescriptive Approaches to Organizational Assessment and Diagnosis

Most organizational assessments look for gaps between *what is* (the actual) and *what should be* (the ideal). But where does the ideal come from? In a *descriptive approach*, ideals come from managers and other stakeholders. In a *prescriptive approach*, ideals come from third-party standards such as best practice studies, surveys of typical business practices, or programs such as Lean Six Sigma, the Malcom Baldrige National Quality Award, Lean Manufacturing, or other statements that articulate how organizations should be. Organizational assessment may compare the organization's current condition (actual) to criteria (ideals) from internal groups or from external sources.

A simple example may illustrate. Some OD practitioners are asked to conduct HR audits, in which the organization can be assessed for its HR practices. One way to conduct an HR audit is to rely on common business practices in HR. A book exists that makes this easy, because a researcher examined many organizational HR systems, and identified how HR departments should carry out their work. Using that book, which comprises a yes or no checklist of several hundred pages, OD practitioners can simply ask HR practitioners in an organization if they do each of the items on the checklist. Any item checked *no* indicates a deficiency that should be addressed. Using the book is a prescriptive approach.

But an HR audit can also be conducted using a descriptive approach. For instance, an OD practitioner may conduct interviews or focus groups with many stakeholders, posing simple questions:

■ What is your organization's HR department doing especially well?
■ What should your organization's HR department do to improve?
■ What is the major strength of the way your organization manages people?

The results of these interviews or focus groups are then analyzed for common themes. The themes represent the description of the situation, indicating gaps for action, when fed back to stakeholders and confirmed.

In the future, look for OD practitioners to combine and integrate these approaches more effectively.

Table 9.1   A Worksheet for Meeting Future Challenges in Organizational Assessment and Diagnosis

Directions: Use this worksheet to plan for meeting future challenges in OD organizational assessment and diagnosis. For each possible trend in the left column below, describe how you plan to meet the challenge in the right column.

Possible Trends in Organizational Assessment and Diagnosis		*How Do You Plan To Meet the Challenge?*
1	OD will face increasing challenges as people grow weary from too many and too frequent assessment efforts	
2	Assessment and diagnosis will be conducted faster using mobile technology	
3	Assessment and diagnosis methods will turn as much to spurring innovation as to identifying problems or leveraging strengths	
4	The importance of trust will grow more apparent in conducting useful organizational assessment and diagnosis	
5	Group decision support systems and collaboration software will make it easier to encourage organizational assessment and diagnosis	
6	Big data will make it easier to collect data about organizational assessment and diagnosis from secondary sources	
7	Internal and external OD practitioners will become more sophisticated in their approaches to conducting organizational assessment and diagnosis	
8	Organizational stakeholders will become more assertive about having a say in organizational assessment and diagnosis	
9	Empirical research will reveal the most important issues to examine when conducting organizational assessment and diagnosis	
10	More efforts will be made to integrate descriptive and prescriptive approaches to organizational assessment and diagnosis	

9.11 Chapter Summary

This book has summarized how OD practitioners can and should conduct organizational assessment and diagnosis. The chapter offered 10 predictions for the future. Use the worksheet appearing in Exhibit 9-1 to structure your thinking on how to prepare for these trends.

Bibliography

Holsapple, C., and Whinston, A. 1996. *Decision Support Systems: A Knowledge Based Approach* (10th ed.). Stavenger, Norway: West group.

Index

Note: Page numbers followed by f and t refer to figures and tables, respectively.

Printed in the United States
by Baker & Taylor Publisher Services